Attachment Theory in the Workplace

Understanding Human Dynamics to Lead, Collaborate, and Thrive

Sacha Vauclair

Introduction: Understanding Attachment and Workplace Dynamics

In today's increasingly complex professional environments, the factors that determine success are often intangible. Beyond technical expertise, strategic planning, and organizational resources, the quality of relationships within a workplace can significantly influence outcomes. Teams that communicate openly, trust one another, and foster mutual respect outperform those that are hindered by interpersonal conflicts, mistrust, and emotional disengagement. However, the mechanisms behind these relational dynamics are frequently misunderstood or overlooked, treated as mere byproducts of personality differences or workplace culture.

Attachment theory offers a transformative perspective for understanding these interactions. Developed by John Bowlby in the mid-20th century and expanded by Mary Ainsworth, attachment theory explores how early bonds with caregivers shape our internal working models of relationships. These models influence how we navigate trust, conflict, and closeness in all aspects of life, including professional settings. Though initially rooted in developmental psychology, the theory has evolved to explain adult behavior, including how individuals relate to colleagues, leaders, and teams.

Every interaction in the workplace, from a casual conversation in the hallway to a high-stakes meeting, is influenced by these attachment-driven tendencies. For example, a manager's reluctance to provide constructive feedback might stem from an avoidant attachment style, characterized by discomfort with vulnerability and emotional confrontation. Similarly, a team member's persistent need for validation and reassurance may reflect an anxious attachment style. Recognizing and addressing these patterns is not just a matter of improving interpersonal dynamics; it is a key to unlocking organizational potential.

Attachment Theory and Its Relevance in the Professional World

Attachment theory is grounded in the premise that humans are inherently social beings. Our early experiences with caregivers shape our understanding of safety, trust, and connection, forming a blueprint for how we approach relationships throughout life. These patterns manifest in adulthood as attachment styles: secure, anxious, avoidant, and disorganized. Each style represents a unique way of managing emotional closeness, dependency, and conflict.

In the workplace, these attachment styles can play out in subtle yet powerful ways. A leader with a secure attachment style may foster an environment where employees feel empowered to take risks and express their ideas without fear of judgment. Conversely, a colleague with an avoidant attachment style may resist collaboration, perceiving it as a threat to their autonomy. An anxious employee might misinterpret neutral feedback as criticism, leading to overcompensation or emotional exhaustion.

These dynamics, while often unconscious, ripple through teams and organizations. They influence how feedback is given and received, how trust is built and maintained, and how conflicts are addressed. Understanding attachment theory provides a framework for decoding these behaviors and responding to them effectively, paving the way for healthier, more productive relationships at work.

Attachment theory becomes particularly relevant in the modern workplace, where rapid technological advancements, evolving work arrangements, and increasing diversity challenge traditional ways of building relationships. The shift to hybrid and remote work has transformed how teams interact, often stripping away the nonverbal cues and casual conversations that previously helped to establish trust. In this context, unresolved attachment dynamics can become even more pronounced, influencing how employees and leaders navigate these new realities.

For instance, consider a remote team where communication relies primarily on digital tools. An employee with an anxious attachment style might feel increasingly disconnected, interpreting delayed responses or limited interactions as signs of disapproval or exclusion. Conversely, a colleague with an avoidant attachment style might thrive in this environment, enjoying the independence it offers, but could become resistant to participating in team-building activities that foster connection. Without an understanding of these underlying attachment styles, leaders may misinterpret these behaviors, attributing them to a lack of commitment or motivation rather than deeper emotional patterns.

Similarly, the increasing emphasis on diversity and inclusion in the workplace introduces new opportunities and challenges. While diverse teams bring rich perspectives and creative problem-solving capabilities, they can also highlight cultural differences in communication, hierarchy, and relational expectations. Attachment theory provides a universal framework for understanding these differences, enabling leaders and teams to approach them with empathy and adaptability. By recognizing and addressing attachment-related needs, organizations can create environments where every individual feels valued and included.

The Role of Emotional Safety in Workplace Success

At the core of attachment theory lies the concept of emotional safety: the belief that one can express thoughts, emotions, and ideas without fear of negative consequences. This foundational element is crucial for fostering trust, innovation, and collaboration in any workplace. Teams that operate with high levels of emotional safety are more likely to take risks, share feedback openly, and recover quickly from setbacks. In contrast, a lack of emotional safety can lead to defensiveness, disengagement, and reduced performance.

Research by Amy Edmondson on psychological safety aligns closely with the principles of attachment theory. Edmondson's studies reveal that teams with psychological safety are better equipped to learn from mistakes, adapt to change, and innovate. Attachment theory deepens this understanding by examining the relational patterns that contribute to—or detract from—psychological safety. For example, leaders with secure attachment styles are more likely to model behaviors that foster emotional safety, such as active listening, consistent communication, and a willingness to acknowledge their own vulnerabilities.

Insecure attachment styles, on the other hand, can undermine emotional safety in subtle but impactful ways. A manager with an avoidant attachment style may struggle to provide emotional support or constructive feedback, leading team members to feel overlooked or undervalued. Similarly, a colleague with a disorganized attachment style might alternate between seeking closeness and pushing others away, creating confusion and tension within the team. Understanding these dynamics allows organizations to proactively address barriers to emotional safety and cultivate a culture of trust and openness.

The significance of emotional safety extends beyond individual relationships. It shapes the broader culture of an organization and directly impacts its ability to perform and innovate. In workplaces where emotional safety is prioritized, employees feel empowered to voice their ideas, challenge assumptions, and take calculated risks without fear of retaliation. This environment not only fosters personal and professional growth but also drives organizational success.

Attachment theory offers actionable insights for creating such environments. Leaders who understand the emotional needs of their teams can implement practices that reinforce trust and collaboration. For example, recognizing that an employee with an anxious attachment style might overanalyze feedback allows a manager to communicate more clearly and affirmatively. Similarly, understanding that avoidant tendencies may lead certain individuals to disengage during high-stress periods equips leaders to re-engage them without triggering defensiveness.

These principles also have profound implications for conflict resolution. Workplace conflicts are often treated as isolated incidents, but they frequently stem from deeper relational patterns linked to attachment styles. For instance, an anxious employee might interpret a colleague's terse email as a personal slight, escalating a minor misunderstanding into a prolonged dispute. Conversely, an avoidant leader might delay addressing the issue altogether, hoping it resolves on its own. Attachment theory encourages a proactive approach, helping teams and leaders address the root causes of conflict and build stronger, more resilient relationships.

Bringing Attachment Theory into the Modern Workplace

Modern workplace challenges demand solutions that address the human side of business. The traditional focus on technical skills and efficiency must now be balanced with an understanding of emotional intelligence and relational dynamics. Attachment theory provides a framework for this balance, offering tools to navigate the complexities of today's professional environments.

In hybrid and remote work settings, attachment-informed practices can bridge the emotional gaps created by physical distance. Regular check-ins, transparent communication, and intentional team-building activities help maintain connections and foster a sense of belonging. For teams spread across cultures and time zones, attachment theory offers a universal language for understanding emotional needs, enabling leaders to create inclusive and supportive environments.

Furthermore, as workplaces become more technology-driven, the principles of attachment theory can help organizations humanize their processes. While automation and artificial intelligence streamline operations, they often reduce opportunities for authentic connection. Leaders who prioritize relational dynamics ensure that employees continue to feel valued and heard, even in highly digitized environments. This balance between innovation and emotional connection is essential for maintaining engagement and morale in the modern workplace.

The relevance of attachment theory is not limited to resolving current workplace challenges. It also provides a vision for the future of professional relationships. As work environments continue to evolve, organizations will increasingly rely on emotional intelligence and relational skills to navigate complexity and uncertainty. Leaders, managers, and employees alike will need to adapt to new norms of collaboration, inclusion, and innovation.

One of the most promising applications of attachment theory lies in leadership development. Effective leadership requires more than technical competence; it demands an ability to inspire trust, manage conflicts constructively, and foster a sense of purpose within teams. Leaders with secure attachment styles naturally exhibit these qualities, but those with insecure tendencies can also develop them through self-awareness and intentional practice. By incorporating attachment-based training into leadership programs, organizations can cultivate emotionally intelligent leaders capable of guiding their teams through both opportunities and challenges.

Attachment theory also offers unique insights into diversity and inclusion initiatives. While these programs often focus on demographic representation, they can be enhanced by addressing the relational dynamics that affect inclusion. For example, understanding how attachment styles influence group dynamics can help leaders create environments where all employees feel genuinely valued and respected. This deeper approach ensures that inclusion goes beyond surface-level metrics, fostering a culture of belonging that drives both engagement and performance.

Looking Ahead

As you embark on this journey, you will explore the profound ways in which attachment theory shapes workplace dynamics. The chapters that follow will provide a comprehensive understanding of attachment styles and their implications for communication, leadership, conflict resolution, and beyond. Through this exploration, you will gain the tools to recognize and address the relational patterns that influence your professional life, empowering you to create stronger, more secure relationships at work.

The insights in this book are not just theoretical; they are practical and actionable. Whether you are a leader seeking to inspire your team, a manager striving to build trust, or an employee navigating challenging relationships, the principles of attachment theory will guide you toward greater understanding and success.

Chapter 1: What Is Attachment Theory?

Attachment theory provides a profound framework for understanding how humans form and sustain relationships. Originally developed by British psychologist John Bowlby in the mid-20th century, attachment theory posits that our early interactions with caregivers lay the foundation for how we connect with others throughout life. These early bonds create internal working models—mental representations of relationships—that influence how we perceive ourselves and others in relational contexts. While the theory was initially designed to explain child-parent dynamics, its relevance has expanded to encompass romantic relationships, friendships, and, more recently, professional interactions.

The core premise of attachment theory is that humans are inherently social beings. From birth, we are wired to seek proximity to others, particularly during times of stress or uncertainty. This need for connection is not merely emotional but also biological, rooted in evolutionary mechanisms that promote survival. A child who can form a secure bond with a caregiver is more likely to receive protection, nourishment, and support. These attachment behaviors, such as seeking closeness, protesting separation, or exploring the environment when safety is assured, are not random but purposeful strategies to maintain proximity to attachment figures.

Bowlby's groundbreaking work introduced the concept of the attachment system, a universal mechanism that governs how individuals form and maintain relationships. His research was further refined by Mary Ainsworth, an American psychologist who developed the "Strange Situation" experiment to classify different attachment styles. These styles—secure, anxious, avoidant, and disorganized—reflect varying patterns of behavior in response to attachment needs. Each style represents a unique strategy for balancing the desire for closeness with the fear of rejection or abandonment.

The Foundations of Attachment Styles

Attachment styles are not inherent traits but learned patterns that emerge from early interactions with caregivers. A child whose caregiver is consistently responsive and nurturing is likely to develop a secure attachment style, characterized by trust, confidence, and the ability to form healthy relationships. Conversely, inconsistent or neglectful caregiving can lead to insecure attachment styles, such as anxious or avoidant. These styles serve as adaptive responses to the relational environment, enabling the child to maximize the likelihood of receiving care despite challenges.

Anxious attachment arises when a caregiver is unpredictable or inconsistently available. The child learns to amplify their emotional expressions—crying louder, clinging harder—to gain attention and reassurance. This hyperactivation of the attachment system fosters a heightened sensitivity to relational cues, often resulting in a preoccupation with closeness and fear of rejection.

Avoidant attachment, on the other hand, develops when a caregiver is consistently unavailable or dismissive. To minimize the pain of unmet needs, the child suppresses their emotional expressions and learns to rely on themselves. This deactivation of the attachment system creates a preference for independence and emotional distance, often accompanied by discomfort with vulnerability.

The disorganized attachment style, the most complex and least common, emerges in environments of fear or trauma. When the caregiver is both a source of comfort and a source of threat, the child experiences a conflict between seeking closeness and avoiding harm. This style is characterized by contradictory behaviors and difficulty forming coherent relational strategies.

Attachment theory, while initially focused on childhood development, has profound implications for adult relationships. The internal working models formed during early life act as blueprints that guide how we approach intimacy, trust, and dependence in adulthood. These patterns are not static; they evolve as we encounter new experiences and relationships. However, the attachment styles we develop as children often create a default mode of relating, which can influence everything from romantic partnerships to professional dynamics.

In the workplace, attachment styles manifest in behaviors that may initially seem unrelated to early relational experiences. For instance, an employee who seeks constant reassurance from their manager may unconsciously replay patterns learned in childhood. Similarly, a leader who avoids giving feedback might be exhibiting avoidant attachment tendencies, rooted in discomfort with confrontation and emotional expression. By understanding these underlying dynamics, professionals can move beyond surface-level interpretations of behavior to address the relational needs driving them.

The concept of secure attachment is particularly important in professional settings. Individuals with secure attachment styles tend to approach relationships with confidence and openness. They are comfortable with both closeness and independence, making them effective collaborators and leaders. These individuals are likely to build trust within teams, handle conflicts constructively, and adapt to challenges with resilience.

Insecure attachment styles, by contrast, often create obstacles in workplace relationships. Anxiously attached employees may overanalyze interactions, misinterpreting neutral feedback as criticism. They might also struggle with boundaries, seeking constant validation from colleagues or supervisors. Avoidantly attached individuals, meanwhile, may prioritize tasks over relationships, withdrawing from team activities or resisting collaboration. While these behaviors may initially appear as personality quirks or professional preferences, they often reflect deeper emotional patterns tied to attachment dynamics.

Disorganized attachment, though less common, can have significant implications in high-stress professional environments. Individuals with this style may exhibit erratic behavior, alternating between seeking support and pushing others away. This unpredictability can create tension within teams, particularly when roles and expectations are unclear. Recognizing and addressing these patterns is essential for fostering a workplace culture of trust and emotional safety.

The Evolution of Attachment Theory

Since its inception, attachment theory has expanded beyond its developmental roots to address a wide range of relational contexts. Bowlby's early work emphasized the biological basis of attachment, highlighting its role in survival and adaptation. However, subsequent research has explored its psychological, emotional, and social dimensions, demonstrating its relevance across cultures and life stages.

Mary Ainsworth's contributions, particularly her identification of attachment styles, laid the groundwork for decades of further study. Researchers such as Hazan and Shaver extended these ideas to adult relationships, exploring how attachment styles influence romantic partnerships, friendships, and even professional interactions. Their work revealed that the patterns established in early life continue to shape our relational behaviors, providing a framework for understanding both harmony and conflict in adult relationships.

Attachment theory has also been enriched by cross-cultural studies, which have highlighted both its universal principles and its cultural variations. While the need for connection and security is a human constant, the ways in which attachment behaviors are expressed and interpreted can vary widely across societies. These insights are particularly relevant in today's globalized workplace, where cultural diversity adds both complexity and richness to relational dynamics.

Attachment theory's extension into adult relationships marked a turning point in understanding human behavior. The work of Hazan and Shaver in the 1980s bridged the gap between developmental psychology and adult relational patterns, demonstrating how attachment styles influence trust, intimacy, and emotional regulation in adulthood. Their findings opened new avenues for research, including the application of attachment theory in professional environments, where collaboration, leadership, and conflict resolution are deeply influenced by relational dynamics.

In the workplace, secure attachment serves as a foundation for effective relationships and productive teams. Employees with secure attachment are typically more adaptable to change, open to feedback, and capable of balancing independence with collaboration. These individuals are likely to approach challenges with confidence, seek support when needed, and contribute constructively to team dynamics. Leaders with secure attachment are often perceived as approachable and trustworthy, fostering a culture of emotional safety that enhances creativity and engagement.

However, the prevalence of insecure attachment styles presents unique challenges in professional settings. Anxious attachment, characterized by a heightened sensitivity to relational cues, can lead to behaviors such as excessive reassurance-seeking or difficulty handling constructive criticism. These patterns, while rooted in a desire for connection, can create strain in professional relationships, particularly in high-pressure environments.

Avoidant attachment, on the other hand, manifests as a preference for emotional distance and self-reliance. Employees with avoidant tendencies may struggle to engage fully in collaborative efforts, perceiving them as intrusive or unnecessary. They may also avoid addressing interpersonal issues, allowing tensions to fester and undermine team cohesion. Leaders with avoidant attachment styles often prioritize tasks over relationships, creating an environment where employees feel unsupported or undervalued.

Disorganized attachment adds another layer of complexity. This style, often linked to unresolved trauma or inconsistent caregiving, is characterized by conflicting impulses to seek and avoid connection. In professional settings, individuals with disorganized attachment may alternate between dependence and withdrawal, creating uncertainty within teams. Their behaviors can be challenging to predict or interpret, requiring a nuanced and empathetic approach from colleagues and leaders.

The Science Behind Attachment in the Workplace

Recent studies have reinforced the relevance of attachment theory in understanding workplace dynamics. Research has shown that attachment styles influence not only individual behaviors but also broader organizational outcomes. For example, teams with high proportions of securely attached members tend to exhibit greater trust, cohesion, and resilience. These teams are better equipped to navigate conflict, adapt to change, and achieve their goals.

In contrast, the presence of unresolved attachment-related tensions can hinder organizational performance. Anxious tendencies may lead to overcommunication or micromanagement, while avoidant tendencies can result in disengagement or resistance to feedback. Disorganized patterns, though less common, can disrupt team stability, particularly in high-stress scenarios.

Understanding these dynamics is essential for creating workplaces that prioritize emotional safety and psychological well-being. Attachment-informed practices, such as clear communication, consistent feedback, and empathetic leadership, can mitigate the impact of insecure attachment styles while fostering a culture of trust and collaboration. By addressing the emotional needs of employees, organizations can unlock their full potential and achieve sustainable success.

Attachment theory's application in professional settings represents a paradigm shift in how we understand workplace dynamics. Traditionally, workplace behavior has been analyzed through the lenses of organizational psychology, leadership theory, and team management frameworks. While these approaches offer valuable insights, they often overlook the deeply rooted emotional patterns that influence how individuals interact within these structures. Attachment theory bridges this gap by focusing on the underlying relational dynamics that drive workplace behaviors.

One of the most significant contributions of attachment theory to the workplace is its ability to explain why individuals respond differently to similar situations. Consider a high-stakes project where team members must collaborate under tight deadlines. A securely attached individual is likely to view this challenge as an opportunity for growth, seeking support and offering it in return. An anxiously attached colleague, however, may interpret the pressure as a threat to their standing within the group, leading to overcommunication or a heightened fear of failure. Meanwhile, an avoidantly attached team member might withdraw, focusing solely on their assigned tasks and avoiding deeper engagement with the team. Disorganized attachment could manifest as erratic behavior, with alternating periods of intense involvement and abrupt disengagement.

Recognizing these patterns allows organizations to respond with tailored strategies that address the specific needs of their employees. For instance, providing clear expectations and regular check-ins can reassure anxiously attached individuals, reducing their stress and enhancing their performance. Encouraging structured but nonintrusive collaboration can help avoidantly attached employees feel more comfortable engaging with their teams. Leaders equipped with an understanding of attachment dynamics are better positioned to navigate these complexities, fostering a culture where every individual can thrive.

Implications for Leadership and Organizational Culture

Attachment theory also has profound implications for leadership development. Effective leaders do more than manage tasks and resources; they cultivate relationships that inspire trust, loyalty, and collaboration. Securely attached leaders naturally excel in these areas, balancing emotional intelligence with strategic decision-making. They create environments where employees feel supported, valued, and empowered to take risks. These leaders model the behaviors they wish to see in their teams, setting a standard for open communication and mutual respect.

For leaders with insecure attachment styles, self-awareness is the first step toward growth. Anxious leaders may need to address their tendencies to overanalyze feedback or seek excessive reassurance. Avoidant leaders might benefit from developing their emotional communication skills, learning to engage with their teams on a deeper level. Disorganized leaders, often grappling with internal conflict, can benefit from coaching or mentorship to develop more consistent and predictable leadership behaviors.

On an organizational level, attachment theory provides a framework for creating cultures that prioritize emotional safety and inclusion. By recognizing the diverse attachment-related needs of their workforce, organizations can implement policies and practices that support trust-building and collaboration. These initiatives might include leadership training programs focused on emotional intelligence, team-building activities designed to foster connection, or conflict resolution processes rooted in empathy and understanding.

The Foundation for a New Workplace Paradigm

Understanding attachment theory is not just an academic exercise—it is a practical tool for transforming workplace relationships. By recognizing the relational patterns that shape behaviors, individuals and organizations can create environments that are both emotionally supportive and highly productive. This chapter has laid the groundwork for exploring these dynamics in greater depth, setting the stage for the practical applications of attachment theory that will be discussed in the chapters to follow.

As you move forward, you will discover how attachment theory influences every aspect of professional life, from communication and leadership to team dynamics and conflict resolution. Armed with this understanding, you will be better equipped to navigate the complexities of modern workplaces, fostering relationships that enhance both individual fulfillment and organizational success.

Chapter 2: Recognizing Attachment Styles at Work

In the complexity of professional environments, the behaviors and reactions of individuals are often attributed to personality, cultural background, or situational factors. While these elements undoubtedly play a role, attachment styles offer an additional, often overlooked, lens through which to understand workplace dynamics. Recognizing attachment styles in ourselves and others is a powerful tool for navigating the challenges of modern work life. It enables professionals to address underlying relational patterns rather than focusing solely on surface-level behaviors.

Attachment styles—secure, anxious, avoidant, and disorganized—are not labels to categorize individuals rigidly. Instead, they represent tendencies or strategies that people use to manage their relational needs. These styles influence how individuals communicate, seek support, handle feedback, and approach conflict. Understanding these dynamics is particularly crucial in environments where collaboration, trust, and adaptability are key to success.

In a workplace setting, attachment styles manifest in a variety of subtle but impactful ways. A manager's reluctance to delegate tasks, for instance, may stem from an anxious attachment style, reflecting a deep-seated fear of being perceived as inadequate. A team member who avoids team meetings might not simply dislike group settings but could be influenced by avoidant tendencies, preferring autonomy over collaboration. Recognizing these patterns requires not only observation but also a willingness to interpret behaviors through the lens of attachment theory.

The Power of Self-Awareness

The journey to recognizing attachment styles in the workplace begins with self-awareness. Understanding your own attachment tendencies is critical for navigating professional relationships effectively. Attachment styles are not static; they can be influenced by life experiences, therapy, and conscious effort. However, without awareness, individuals are likely to operate on autopilot, unconsciously replaying relational patterns learned in childhood.

A person with a secure attachment style is likely to feel confident in their interactions, striking a healthy balance between independence and collaboration. They are comfortable giving and receiving feedback, managing conflicts constructively, and seeking support when needed. In contrast, individuals with insecure attachment styles may struggle with these areas. Anxiously attached professionals might overanalyze interactions, seeking constant validation from colleagues or supervisors. Avoidantly attached individuals might shy away from emotional discussions, focusing exclusively on tasks and deadlines. Disorganized attachment, marked by inconsistency and internal conflict, can lead to unpredictable behaviors that challenge team dynamics.

Self-awareness allows individuals to identify these patterns and take proactive steps to mitigate their negative impacts. For example, an anxious employee who recognizes their tendency to seek excessive reassurance might work on building internal confidence. Similarly, an avoidant manager who understands their discomfort with emotional expression can practice small steps toward vulnerability, such as acknowledging a team member's efforts or emotions.

Understanding the attachment styles of colleagues and leaders is as critical as self-awareness in creating harmonious and productive workplace relationships. While attachment styles are not always overt, their effects often emerge through consistent patterns of behavior. Observing how individuals approach collaboration, handle feedback, and manage conflict can provide valuable insights into their underlying relational tendencies. Recognizing these dynamics is not about labeling or diagnosing; rather, it is about fostering empathy and creating opportunities for constructive interaction.

In professional settings, secure attachment typically manifests as confidence, adaptability, and openness to feedback. Securely attached individuals are more likely to contribute positively to team dynamics, approaching tasks with a sense of purpose and resilience. Their ability to balance independence with interdependence makes them effective collaborators, and their comfort with vulnerability often translates into clear and constructive communication. Teams with a high proportion of securely attached members tend to exhibit greater trust and cohesion, fostering an environment of emotional safety that benefits all participants.

Anxious attachment, by contrast, can create challenges in the workplace. Professionals with this style may exhibit heightened sensitivity to relational cues, often interpreting neutral or ambiguous interactions as negative. For example, a delayed email response from a colleague might be perceived as a sign of disapproval or exclusion. This heightened emotional reactivity can lead to overcommunication, where anxiously attached individuals seek constant reassurance or validation. While these behaviors stem from a desire to connect, they can strain professional relationships if not managed constructively.

Avoidant attachment presents a different set of challenges. Avoidantly attached individuals often prioritize tasks and goals over relationships, valuing autonomy and self-reliance. While this focus on independence can be an asset in certain roles, it may hinder collaboration and team cohesion. These individuals might resist engaging in open discussions about emotions or relational dynamics, viewing such conversations as unnecessary or uncomfortable. Their reluctance to rely on others can also limit their effectiveness in roles that require interdependence and trust.

Disorganized attachment, though less common, can have significant implications in high-stress professional environments. Individuals with this style often exhibit contradictory behaviors, alternating between seeking closeness and pushing others away. This inconsistency can create confusion within teams, as colleagues struggle to predict or interpret their actions. Disorganized attachment is often rooted in past trauma or unresolved relational conflicts, requiring a nuanced and empathetic approach from managers and peers.

Creating a Workplace Culture of Empathy and Understanding

Recognizing attachment styles is not about assigning blame or fixing individuals. Instead, it is about creating a workplace culture that acknowledges and accommodates the diverse relational needs of its members. Empathy is central to this process. When leaders and colleagues approach workplace behaviors with curiosity rather than judgment, they create opportunities for connection and growth.

For instance, a manager who understands that an employee's need for frequent check-ins stems from an anxious attachment style can provide structured and consistent feedback to address this need without enabling dependency. Similarly, a team member who recognizes a colleague's avoidant tendencies can approach collaboration in ways that respect their preference for autonomy, such as setting clear boundaries and focusing on task-oriented discussions.

This culture of empathy and understanding extends beyond individual relationships to influence organizational practices. Training programs on emotional intelligence and relational dynamics can equip employees at all levels with the tools to navigate attachment-related challenges. Policies that prioritize psychological safety, such as encouraging open dialogue and addressing conflicts proactively, can further reinforce this culture. By integrating attachment-informed practices into the fabric of workplace interactions, organizations can foster environments where both individuals and teams thrive.

Recognizing attachment styles in the workplace involves observing behaviors and understanding the emotional motivations that drive them. While attachment tendencies are often subtle, they manifest consistently in how individuals approach relationships and tasks. For leaders, this awareness is especially critical, as it allows them to navigate team dynamics with greater precision and empathy.

In anxious attachment, the hallmark behaviors often revolve around seeking connection and reassurance. These professionals may be overly attentive to the opinions and moods of their colleagues, fearing rejection or criticism. This hypervigilance can result in behaviors like overexplaining decisions, frequently asking for feedback, or interpreting minor setbacks as major failures. While their intentions are often rooted in a genuine desire to succeed and belong, their actions can sometimes create unnecessary tension within a team. Managers working with anxiously attached individuals can address these tendencies by offering consistent and constructive feedback, clearly setting expectations, and fostering an inclusive atmosphere where their contributions are valued.

Avoidant attachment, on the other hand, may be less immediately apparent but can pose unique challenges in team settings. Individuals with avoidant tendencies often prioritize self-reliance and autonomy over collaboration. They may resist sharing personal information or engaging in emotionally charged conversations, viewing such exchanges as uncomfortable or unproductive. In team environments, this avoidance can lead to miscommunications or perceptions of disengagement. However, these professionals excel in roles that require independence, focus, and problem-solving. Leaders can support avoidantly attached employees by providing clear objectives, respecting their need for autonomy, and encouraging gradual engagement in relational aspects of their work.

Disorganized attachment is the most complex style to identify and address in professional contexts. These individuals may alternate between behaviors associated with both anxious and avoidant tendencies, creating a pattern of inconsistency that can disrupt team dynamics. For example, they might seek close collaboration one day and withdraw the next, leaving colleagues uncertain about how to engage with them. This unpredictability is often rooted in unresolved internal conflicts, making it challenging to establish trust and consistency. Managers and colleagues can navigate these dynamics by maintaining clear and predictable communication, offering reassurance without overstepping boundaries, and fostering an environment of psychological safety.

Practical Tools for Identifying Attachment Styles

While understanding attachment styles is essential, applying this knowledge requires sensitivity and discretion. The workplace is not a therapeutic setting, and employees may not be aware of their own attachment tendencies. Rather than directly labeling behaviors, leaders and colleagues can use observation and reflective practices to better understand relational dynamics.

For instance, leaders can note patterns in how individuals respond to feedback, approach collaboration, or handle conflict. Do they seem overly concerned with approval? Do they avoid interpersonal discussions, focusing solely on tasks? Do they exhibit inconsistent engagement, alternating between connection and withdrawal? These observations can provide valuable insights into underlying attachment styles without making assumptions or drawing definitive conclusions.

Encouraging open dialogue is another effective strategy. Regular one-on-one meetings, team discussions, and feedback sessions create opportunities for individuals to express their needs and preferences. When leaders approach these conversations with curiosity and empathy, they pave the way for deeper understanding and stronger relationships. For example, a manager might ask, "What type of feedback helps you the most?" or "How can I support you in feeling more confident in your role?" These questions invite reflection and collaboration, fostering trust and mutual respect.

Recognizing attachment styles is not an end in itself but a foundation for building stronger, more resilient workplace relationships. By understanding how attachment dynamics influence behaviors, leaders and teams can develop strategies to address challenges and foster a more inclusive and emotionally supportive environment. This process requires both a commitment to self-awareness and an openness to understanding the needs of others.

A critical step in integrating attachment theory into workplace practices is fostering a culture of emotional safety. Emotional safety creates the conditions for individuals to express themselves authentically without fear of judgment or reprisal. This is particularly important for individuals with insecure attachment styles, who may be more sensitive to perceived rejection or criticism. In a workplace where emotional safety is prioritized, anxiously attached employees feel reassured, avoidant employees feel respected, and disorganized employees find stability. This shared sense of safety enables teams to collaborate more effectively, resolve conflicts constructively, and innovate with confidence.

Leadership plays a pivotal role in creating this culture. Securely attached leaders naturally embody behaviors that foster emotional safety, such as active listening, empathetic communication, and consistent feedback. However, leaders with insecure attachment tendencies can also develop these skills through intentional practice. For example, an avoidant leader might work on expressing appreciation for their team's contributions, while an anxious leader might focus on providing clear and concise feedback to avoid overcompensating for perceived gaps in communication. These small but deliberate changes can have a profound impact on team dynamics and overall morale.

The Benefits of Attachment-Informed Practices

Organizations that integrate attachment theory into their leadership and team-building strategies often experience tangible benefits. Teams with a strong foundation of trust and emotional safety are more resilient in the face of challenges, adapting to change with greater agility and maintaining high levels of engagement. Employees in such environments report higher job satisfaction, stronger connections with their colleagues, and a greater sense of purpose in their work.

Moreover, attachment-informed practices can enhance diversity and inclusion efforts. Recognizing the diverse attachment-related needs of employees allows organizations to create more equitable and supportive environments. For instance, providing flexibility in how employees engage with their work—such as offering a mix of collaborative and independent tasks—ensures that individuals with different relational tendencies can thrive. Similarly, addressing attachment dynamics in leadership training programs equips managers to navigate the complexities of multicultural teams, where cultural differences may intersect with attachment-related behaviors.

A Lens for Understanding Workplace Dynamics

Attachment theory offers a powerful lens for understanding the relational patterns that shape workplace behaviors. By recognizing attachment styles in ourselves and others, we gain the tools to navigate professional relationships with greater empathy, patience, and intentionality. This chapter has explored the foundational concepts of attachment styles as they apply to workplace settings, highlighting both their challenges and their potential for fostering growth.

As you continue reading, you will discover how these insights can be applied to specific aspects of professional life, from communication and collaboration to leadership and conflict resolution. By embracing the principles of attachment theory, you can contribute to a workplace culture that values connection, trust, and emotional resilience, paving the way for both individual and organizational success.

Chapter 3: The Role of Emotional Safety in Professional Relationships

Emotional safety is a foundational element of any successful professional relationship. It underpins trust, collaboration, and innovation, creating the conditions for individuals to express themselves authentically and contribute to their fullest potential. In the absence of emotional safety, employees are less likely to take risks, share ideas, or engage fully with their teams, leading to a decline in productivity and morale. While often associated with interpersonal relationships outside of work, emotional safety is equally critical in professional environments, where it shapes the culture, dynamics, and outcomes of organizations.

The concept of emotional safety can be traced to the broader framework of psychological safety, a term popularized by organizational behavior scholar Amy Edmondson. Psychological safety refers to a shared belief that a team is a safe space for interpersonal risk-taking. When employees feel psychologically safe, they are more likely to speak up, admit mistakes, and seek feedback without fear of negative consequences. Attachment theory enriches this understanding by providing insights into the relational patterns that either support or undermine emotional safety.

At its core, emotional safety is about connection. It arises when individuals feel valued, understood, and respected in their relationships. In the workplace, this means creating environments where employees can trust that their contributions will be acknowledged and their concerns addressed. Emotional safety does not imply the absence of conflict or discomfort; rather, it ensures that such challenges can be navigated constructively, without threatening the dignity or security of those involved.

Attachment Theory and Emotional Safety

Attachment theory offers a powerful lens for understanding the conditions that foster or hinder emotional safety. Secure attachment is characterized by a sense of confidence in one's relationships, enabling individuals to engage with others openly and constructively. In the workplace, securely attached employees are more likely to feel comfortable expressing their ideas, seeking support, and collaborating with colleagues. Their sense of security provides a stable foundation for building trust and navigating challenges.

Insecure attachment styles, on the other hand, can create barriers to emotional safety. Anxiously attached individuals may struggle to feel secure in their relationships, constantly seeking reassurance or validation from colleagues and leaders. This heightened sensitivity can lead to misunderstandings and conflicts, particularly in environments where feedback is ambiguous or inconsistent. Avoidantly attached employees, by contrast, may disengage from relational aspects of work altogether, focusing solely on tasks and avoiding deeper connections. While this strategy may protect them from perceived vulnerabilities, it can also limit their ability to contribute fully to team dynamics.

Disorganized attachment, which combines elements of both anxiety and avoidance, presents unique challenges in fostering emotional safety. Individuals with this style may exhibit contradictory behaviors, such as seeking closeness while simultaneously pushing others away. Their unpredictability can create tension within teams, making it difficult to establish consistent and trusting relationships.

Recognizing these patterns is the first step in creating a workplace culture that prioritizes emotional safety. By understanding the relational needs of employees and addressing their concerns empathetically, organizations can foster environments where individuals feel supported and empowered.

Emotional safety is not merely a desirable quality in workplace relationships; it is a strategic imperative. Research consistently demonstrates that organizations with high levels of emotional and psychological safety outperform those without it. Employees in such environments are more engaged, creative, and resilient, enabling teams to adapt quickly to challenges and seize opportunities. Moreover, emotional safety is linked to higher job satisfaction and reduced turnover, as employees are more likely to remain committed to organizations where they feel valued and secure.

Attachment theory provides a framework for understanding the relational dynamics that contribute to emotional safety. Securely attached individuals naturally model behaviors that promote trust and connection, such as active listening, constructive feedback, and collaborative problem-solving. Their presence in a team or organization sets the tone for others, creating a ripple effect that reinforces positive relational dynamics.

Conversely, insecure attachment styles can introduce challenges to emotional safety. Anxiously attached employees, for instance, may misinterpret neutral feedback as criticism, leading to heightened emotional responses that can strain relationships. Their need for validation may also manifest as overcommunication, which, if not managed constructively, can overwhelm colleagues. Avoidantly attached individuals, on the other hand, may resist efforts to build rapport or address conflicts, viewing such interactions as unnecessary or intrusive. Their reluctance to engage emotionally can hinder trust and collaboration, particularly in team-based settings.

Understanding these dynamics allows leaders and teams to take proactive steps toward fostering emotional safety. One key strategy is to establish clear communication norms that promote openness and respect. For example, creating structured opportunities for feedback—such as regular check-ins or team reviews—can provide a safe space for anxiously attached employees to voice concerns and receive validation. Similarly, offering avoidantly attached individuals autonomy in how they engage with others can help them feel more comfortable participating in relational aspects of work.

Building Trust Through Emotional Safety

Trust is the cornerstone of emotional safety, and attachment theory offers valuable insights into how trust is built and maintained. Securely attached individuals are naturally inclined to trust others, as their internal working models are rooted in the expectation of reliability and support. This trust enables them to approach relationships with openness and confidence, fostering a positive cycle of mutual respect and cooperation.

Insecure attachment styles, however, can complicate the process of building trust. Anxiously attached individuals may struggle to trust others fully, fearing rejection or abandonment. Their heightened vigilance can lead to behaviors such as second-guessing colleagues' intentions or seeking constant reassurance. Avoidantly attached individuals, by contrast, may be reluctant to extend trust, preferring to rely on themselves rather than risk vulnerability. Disorganized attachment adds further complexity, as these individuals may oscillate between trust and mistrust, creating unpredictability in their relationships.

Leaders play a critical role in establishing trust within their teams. By demonstrating consistency, transparency, and empathy, they can create an environment where employees feel secure. For instance, leaders who follow through on commitments and communicate openly about challenges build credibility, reassuring anxiously attached employees. Similarly, providing clear expectations and respecting boundaries helps avoidantly attached individuals feel more at ease, reducing resistance to collaboration.

Trust-building is not a one-time effort but an ongoing process. Regular opportunities for dialogue, recognition of contributions, and the resolution of conflicts in a fair and respectful manner all contribute to maintaining emotional safety. Organizations that prioritize trust-building at every level create cultures where employees feel supported and valued, paving the way for long-term success.

The ripple effects of emotional safety extend beyond individual relationships to shape the overall culture of an organization. When emotional safety is prioritized, employees are not only more likely to engage authentically but also to take calculated risks, share innovative ideas, and recover quickly from setbacks. This cultural dynamic fosters a sense of collective resilience, enabling teams to thrive even in high-pressure or uncertain environments.

Attachment theory helps illuminate why emotional safety is essential for organizational success. Insecurely attached individuals, whether anxious, avoidant, or disorganized, often experience heightened stress in the absence of emotional safety. This stress can manifest in behaviors that disrupt team dynamics, such as defensiveness, withdrawal, or overdependence on authority figures. Securely attached individuals, by contrast, provide stability and a sense of calm, helping to balance and counteract these tendencies within a group.

For teams to function optimally, leaders must recognize and address the attachment-related needs of their members. For example, anxiously attached employees may benefit from consistent feedback and clear communication, which can alleviate their fear of rejection. Avoidantly attached colleagues, on the other hand, might need space to process information independently before engaging in collaborative discussions. By tailoring their approach to the diverse needs of their teams, leaders can create an inclusive environment that supports emotional safety for all.

Conflict Resolution and Emotional Safety

Conflict is an inevitable part of professional life, but the way it is managed can either reinforce or undermine emotional safety. Attachment theory provides valuable insights into how individuals with different attachment styles approach conflict, shedding light on the underlying motivations and fears that drive their behavior.

Anxiously attached individuals often view conflict as a threat to the relationship itself, leading them to either avoid confrontation altogether or escalate the situation in an effort to secure reassurance. Their heightened sensitivity to perceived rejection can make even minor disagreements feel disproportionately significant. Avoidantly attached individuals, by contrast, are likely to disengage from conflict, minimizing its importance or refusing to address it directly. This avoidance may stem from a fear of vulnerability or a desire to maintain emotional distance. Disorganized attachment complicates matters further, as these individuals may exhibit erratic behaviors during conflict, oscillating between aggression and withdrawal.

Leaders and teams can foster emotional safety during conflicts by adopting attachment-informed strategies. For instance, creating a structured process for addressing disagreements—such as facilitated discussions or mediation—provides a safe space for anxiously attached individuals to express their concerns without fear of judgment. Encouraging avoidantly attached employees to participate in conflict resolution discussions at their own pace can help them engage without feeling overwhelmed. For those with disorganized attachment tendencies, offering reassurance and clear guidelines can reduce the unpredictability of their responses.

Ultimately, conflict resolution in an emotionally safe environment is not about eliminating disagreement but about navigating it constructively. When teams address conflicts with empathy and respect, they strengthen their relationships and build trust, reinforcing the foundation of emotional safety.

Creating and maintaining emotional safety is not a static goal but an ongoing process that evolves with the needs of the team and the organization. Emotional safety is closely tied to the broader concept of psychological safety, which encompasses not only interpersonal trust but also a sense of inclusion and belonging. This integration is particularly important in today's professional landscape, where diverse teams, hybrid work environments, and rapid change require a deeper commitment to relational understanding.

Leaders have a unique role in fostering emotional safety. Their behaviors, decisions, and communication styles set the tone for the entire team. A leader who models vulnerability—acknowledging mistakes, seeking feedback, and sharing their own challenges—creates an environment where employees feel safe to do the same. This openness is particularly impactful for employees with insecure attachment styles, who may need additional reassurance to feel confident in their contributions.

Organizations can institutionalize emotional safety through policies and practices that prioritize relational health. Regular team-building activities, inclusive decision-making processes, and consistent performance reviews are just a few examples of initiatives that reinforce trust and connection. Training programs that focus on emotional intelligence and attachment-informed leadership provide leaders and employees with the tools to navigate relational dynamics effectively. These practices signal to employees that their emotional well-being is valued, which, in turn, enhances engagement and loyalty.

The Transformative Power of Emotional Safety

The benefits of emotional safety extend beyond individual and team performance to influence the overall success and resilience of an organization. Teams that operate with high levels of emotional safety are more adaptable to change, better equipped to handle crises, and more likely to innovate. These advantages are not just theoretical; they are supported by empirical research. Studies show that organizations with psychologically safe cultures experience higher retention rates, stronger financial performance, and greater employee satisfaction.

Attachment theory deepens our understanding of why these outcomes occur. By addressing the relational needs of employees, organizations create environments where individuals feel empowered to take risks, voice their ideas, and collaborate effectively. This relational foundation is particularly important in times of uncertainty or stress, when the ability to trust and rely on one another becomes critical.

However, achieving and sustaining emotional safety requires a long-term commitment. It involves not only addressing immediate challenges but also anticipating and adapting to future needs. As workplaces continue to evolve—embracing remote work, technological advancements, and increasing diversity—the principles of attachment theory will remain a valuable guide for fostering emotional safety and connection.

Emotional Safety as a Catalyst for Success

Emotional safety is more than a desirable quality in professional relationships—it is a catalyst for individual and organizational success. By understanding the role of attachment styles in shaping workplace behaviors, leaders and teams can create environments that prioritize trust, respect, and empathy. This chapter has explored the critical importance of emotional safety, offering insights into how attachment-informed practices can enhance communication, collaboration, and conflict resolution.

As we move forward in this book, we will delve deeper into the practical applications of these principles, examining how they influence leadership, team dynamics, and organizational culture. By embracing emotional safety as a core value, professionals at all levels can contribute to workplaces that are not only more effective but also more humane.

Chapter 4: Attachment Styles and Communication

Communication is the backbone of every professional relationship, shaping how individuals collaborate, solve problems, and build trust. Despite its centrality in workplace dynamics, effective communication often remains elusive, hindered by misinterpretations, conflicting expectations, or unresolved tensions. Attachment theory provides a nuanced framework for understanding these challenges, revealing how deep-seated relational patterns influence the way people exchange information and emotions.

Attachment styles—secure, anxious, avoidant, and disorganized—significantly impact communication behaviors. Each style reflects a unique approach to managing emotional closeness, vulnerability, and conflict, influencing not only what is communicated but also how it is received and interpreted. For instance, securely attached individuals tend to communicate openly and constructively, while those with insecure attachment styles may struggle with ambiguity, emotional expression, or feedback. Understanding these tendencies is essential for creating effective and empathetic communication in professional settings.

In workplace environments, communication serves multiple functions: coordinating tasks, resolving conflicts, fostering collaboration, and building relationships. The interplay of attachment styles within these interactions often determines their success or failure. A manager's ability to provide clear and supportive feedback, a colleague's willingness to share ideas in a meeting, or an employee's approach to conflict resolution can all be traced back to underlying attachment dynamics. By recognizing these patterns, professionals can navigate communication challenges with greater empathy and effectiveness.

Secure Attachment and Effective Communication

Securely attached individuals are often considered the gold standard of workplace communication. Their internal working models are rooted in trust and confidence, enabling them to express themselves clearly and listen actively to others. These individuals are comfortable with both giving and receiving feedback, balancing assertiveness with empathy. They approach communication as a means of building connection and understanding, fostering a collaborative and supportive atmosphere.

In team settings, securely attached employees are likely to facilitate open dialogue, encouraging diverse perspectives and creating space for constructive disagreement. Their ability to manage emotional expression and remain composed under pressure makes them valuable mediators during conflicts. Leaders with secure attachment styles model these behaviors for their teams, setting the tone for respectful and effective communication.

The positive influence of securely attached individuals extends beyond their own interactions. Their presence in a team can help buffer the impact of insecure attachment styles, providing stability and reassurance to colleagues who may struggle with communication. For example, a secure manager might help an anxiously attached employee feel more confident by offering consistent and affirmative feedback, or encourage an avoidantly attached team member to participate more fully in discussions.

While secure attachment provides an ideal foundation for communication, insecure attachment styles introduce complexities that can challenge workplace dynamics. Anxious attachment, for instance, is characterized by a heightened sensitivity to relational cues and a strong need for validation. These tendencies often influence how individuals with this style communicate, shaping both the content and tone of their interactions.

Anxiously attached individuals tend to prioritize maintaining relationships, sometimes at the expense of clarity or directness. They may avoid raising concerns or expressing dissent out of fear that such actions will jeopardize their connection with others. Instead, they often seek reassurance through excessive communication, such as frequent emails or repeated requests for feedback. While these behaviors stem from a desire for connection and security, they can overwhelm colleagues or lead to misunderstandings.

In conflict situations, anxious communicators may struggle to regulate their emotions, reacting defensively or escalating minor issues into significant disputes. Their preoccupation with perceived rejection can make them overly reactive to ambiguous or neutral feedback, interpreting it as criticism. For example, a manager's brief email might be read as dismissive, triggering anxiety and prompting a flurry of follow-up questions.

Understanding these patterns allows leaders and colleagues to respond with empathy rather than frustration. Providing clear, consistent communication helps alleviate the fears of anxiously attached individuals, enabling them to feel secure in their professional relationships. Structured opportunities for feedback, such as scheduled one-on-one meetings, can also reduce their need for constant reassurance by establishing predictable channels for interaction.

Avoidant Attachment and the Struggle for Connection

Avoidant attachment presents a different set of challenges in workplace communication. Individuals with this style often prioritize independence and self-reliance, viewing emotional expression as unnecessary or uncomfortable. As a result, they may avoid engaging deeply in conversations that involve vulnerability or interpersonal dynamics, focusing instead on tasks and outcomes.

Avoidantly attached professionals may come across as distant or unapproachable, even when this is not their intention. Their preference for minimal interaction can lead to brief, transactional communication that lacks warmth or nuance. For example, an avoidantly attached manager might deliver feedback in a curt, impersonal manner, inadvertently creating tension or alienation among team members.

This reluctance to engage in relational aspects of communication can hinder collaboration and trust-building. Avoidantly attached individuals may resist participating in team discussions, preferring to work independently or delegate tasks without seeking input. In conflict situations, they are likely to withdraw or disengage rather than address the issue directly, which can leave problems unresolved and frustrations unspoken.

However, avoidantly attached employees often excel in roles that require focus, autonomy, and problem-solving. Recognizing their strengths while addressing their communication challenges is key to integrating them effectively into team dynamics. Leaders can support avoidantly attached individuals by respecting their need for space while encouraging gradual engagement in relational aspects of work. Providing clear expectations and emphasizing the practical benefits of collaboration can help them feel more comfortable participating in discussions and building connections.

Disorganized attachment introduces a unique complexity to workplace communication. Individuals with this style often exhibit contradictory behaviors, reflecting a deep internal conflict between seeking connection and avoiding vulnerability. These tendencies can create unpredictability in their interactions, making it challenging for colleagues and leaders to navigate their communication style effectively.

Disorganized communicators may alternate between intense engagement and abrupt withdrawal. For instance, they might enthusiastically participate in a brainstorming session one day, only to isolate themselves the next. This inconsistency can leave team members uncertain about how to approach them or interpret their behavior. In emotionally charged situations, individuals with disorganized attachment may exhibit heightened reactivity, oscillating between defensive outbursts and avoidance. These patterns are often rooted in unresolved relational trauma, which shapes their internal working models of relationships.

Despite these challenges, individuals with disorganized attachment can contribute significantly to team dynamics when provided with the right support. Clear, predictable communication is essential for creating a sense of stability and trust. Leaders can help by establishing structured routines and offering consistent feedback, which reduces the ambiguity that often triggers insecurity in disorganized communicators. Empathy and patience are also crucial, as these individuals may require more time and reassurance to feel secure in their professional relationships.

Colleagues can play a role in fostering connection by maintaining open and nonjudgmental dialogue. Encouraging collaborative efforts that emphasize shared goals rather than interpersonal dynamics can help disorganized communicators engage more comfortably. Over time, these strategies can build the trust and consistency needed to support their participation and contribution.

Bridging Attachment Styles in Communication

One of the most significant challenges in workplace communication is bridging the differences between attachment styles. Misaligned expectations and behaviors can lead to misunderstandings, frustration, and conflict. For example, an anxiously attached employee might interpret an avoidantly attached colleague's brief responses as disinterest or rejection, while the avoidant individual may view the anxious person's frequent communication as intrusive or overwhelming. These dynamics, if left unaddressed, can create tension that undermines team cohesion and productivity.

Attachment theory offers a framework for navigating these challenges by fostering empathy and understanding. Recognizing that communication behaviors are often driven by underlying relational needs allows professionals to approach interactions with greater sensitivity. For instance, a manager who understands that an anxious team member's frequent check-ins reflect a need for reassurance can respond with patience rather than irritation. Similarly, encouraging an avoidantly attached colleague to share their perspective in a low-pressure setting can help bridge the gap between their preference for independence and the team's need for collaboration.

Building communication bridges requires intentional effort and adaptive strategies. Leaders play a crucial role in modeling inclusive communication practices that accommodate diverse attachment styles. This might involve balancing directness with empathy, providing both clarity and emotional support, and creating opportunities for dialogue that prioritize mutual respect. Teams that embrace these principles are better equipped to navigate differences and foster a culture of trust and collaboration.

The workplace is a dynamic environment where effective communication often determines the success of both individual relationships and broader team objectives. By incorporating the principles of attachment theory, organizations can cultivate communication practices that support trust, understanding, and collaboration across diverse attachment styles. This requires a commitment to empathy, adaptability, and proactive leadership.

One of the most effective ways to enhance workplace communication is to establish clear and consistent norms. Predictability in how messages are delivered, feedback is given, and expectations are communicated creates a sense of stability, particularly for individuals with insecure attachment styles. Structured communication channels, such as regular team meetings or one-on-one check-ins, provide opportunities for employees to voice concerns, seek guidance, and share updates in a supportive environment.

Leaders who model attachment-informed communication set the tone for their teams. This involves demonstrating behaviors that foster trust and emotional safety, such as active listening, validating others' perspectives, and addressing misunderstandings promptly. For example, a leader who acknowledges the unique communication needs of their team members—whether by offering frequent feedback for an anxious employee or allowing space for an avoidantly attached colleague—builds stronger, more resilient relationships.

Team-building initiatives also play a vital role in bridging attachment-related differences in communication. Activities that emphasize shared goals and mutual support help employees understand and appreciate each other's strengths, reducing potential conflicts stemming from mismatched communication styles. By creating opportunities for connection in a low-pressure context, these initiatives encourage open dialogue and foster a sense of belonging.

Communication in High-Stress Scenarios

Stressful situations, such as tight deadlines, organizational changes, or interpersonal conflicts, often amplify the influence of attachment styles on communication. Anxiously attached individuals may become more vocal or demanding, seeking additional reassurance to manage their heightened emotional state. Avoidantly attached colleagues might retreat further into independence, resisting efforts to engage them in collaborative problem-solving. Disorganized communicators may exhibit erratic behaviors, alternating between engagement and withdrawal.

To navigate these dynamics effectively, organizations must prioritize clear, transparent, and empathetic communication during high-stress periods. Leaders should address uncertainties directly, provide regular updates, and invite input from all team members. This approach not only mitigates the impact of stress on communication but also reinforces a culture of trust and inclusivity.

In addition, stress management resources—such as training on emotional intelligence, access to counseling services, or workshops on conflict resolution—equip employees with the tools to regulate their emotional responses and communicate constructively under pressure. These initiatives help normalize discussions around emotional well-being, fostering an environment where individuals feel supported even in challenging circumstances.

The Transformative Power of Attachment-Informed Communication

Attachment theory provides a transformative lens for understanding and improving workplace communication. By recognizing the relational patterns that influence how individuals express themselves and interact with others, professionals can navigate communication challenges with greater empathy and effectiveness. This chapter has explored the diverse ways in which attachment styles shape workplace communication, highlighting both the challenges and opportunities they present.

As the book progresses, these insights will be further applied to specific aspects of professional life, from leadership and team dynamics to conflict resolution and organizational culture. By embracing attachment-informed communication practices, professionals can contribute to a workplace environment that values connection, respect, and collaboration, ultimately enhancing both individual and organizational success.

Chapter 5: Attachment Styles and Leadership

Leadership is often regarded as a blend of vision, decision-making, and the ability to inspire others. While these qualities are essential, they only tell part of the story. The relational dynamics a leader fosters within their team are equally critical to success, influencing everything from morale and productivity to innovation and resilience. Attachment theory offers a valuable framework for understanding how these dynamics are shaped by a leader's attachment style. By examining the relational patterns that leaders bring to their roles, we can uncover the hidden forces that drive their behaviors, decisions, and impact.

Attachment styles—secure, anxious, avoidant, and disorganized—are not confined to personal relationships. They manifest in leadership styles, influencing how individuals approach authority, collaboration, and conflict. A leader's attachment style not only affects their interactions with their team but also sets the tone for the overall workplace culture. Securely attached leaders, for instance, often model behaviors that promote trust, openness, and emotional safety, creating an environment where employees feel empowered to thrive. Conversely, leaders with insecure attachment styles may unintentionally introduce relational challenges that hinder team cohesion and performance.

Understanding these dynamics is not about labeling or judging leaders but about recognizing the relational tendencies that shape their approach. This awareness allows for targeted growth, enabling leaders to leverage their strengths and address potential blind spots. Whether through self-reflection, training, or mentorship, leaders can cultivate attachment-informed practices that enhance their effectiveness and foster healthier workplace relationships.

Secure Attachment and Effective Leadership

Leaders with a secure attachment style are often seen as the gold standard in leadership. Their internal working models are rooted in trust and confidence, enabling them to approach relationships with openness and authenticity. Securely attached leaders are comfortable with both authority and vulnerability, striking a balance that inspires trust and loyalty among their team members.

One of the defining characteristics of securely attached leaders is their ability to create a sense of emotional safety within their teams. They value collaboration and actively seek input from others, recognizing that diverse perspectives enhance decision-making. Their communication style is clear, consistent, and empathetic, fostering an environment where employees feel heard and respected. This relational foundation encourages team members to take risks, share ideas, and engage fully in their work.

In addition to fostering trust, securely attached leaders excel in managing conflict. They approach disagreements constructively, focusing on resolving issues rather than assigning blame. Their ability to regulate their emotions under pressure sets a positive example for their team, reinforcing a culture of respect and accountability. Moreover, their confidence in their own abilities allows them to delegate effectively, empowering employees to take ownership of their responsibilities and develop their skills.

The benefits of secure leadership extend beyond individual relationships. Teams led by securely attached individuals often exhibit higher levels of cohesion, engagement, and resilience. These teams are better equipped to navigate challenges and adapt to change, as their foundation of trust and collaboration provides a buffer against stress and uncertainty.

While secure attachment serves as an ideal foundation for leadership, many leaders exhibit behaviors shaped by insecure attachment styles —anxious, avoidant, or disorganized. These tendencies, often rooted in early relational experiences, influence how leaders navigate authority, relationships, and challenges within their teams. Understanding these dynamics is key to fostering growth and mitigating potential challenges.

Anxiously attached leaders often prioritize relationships above all else, seeking reassurance and approval from their team or superiors. This need for validation can manifest in behaviors such as over-involvement in team tasks, reluctance to delegate, or sensitivity to perceived criticism. For example, an anxious leader may frequently check in on their team's progress, not out of distrust but as a way to soothe their own fears of inadequacy. While their intentions may be positive, these behaviors can inadvertently signal a lack of trust in their team's capabilities, leading to frustration or disengagement among employees.

In conflict situations, anxious leaders may struggle to maintain composure, reacting emotionally or attempting to placate others to restore harmony. Their heightened sensitivity to interpersonal dynamics can make them adept at recognizing and addressing relational issues, but it can also leave them vulnerable to burnout or decision paralysis. To thrive as leaders, individuals with anxious attachment tendencies can benefit from developing self-regulation skills, such as mindfulness or stress management techniques, and seeking constructive feedback to build confidence in their decision-making abilities.

Avoidant Attachment and Leadership Challenges

Leaders with avoidant attachment styles often approach their roles with a strong emphasis on independence and self-reliance. While these qualities can be assets in certain contexts, they may also hinder their ability to engage deeply with their team. Avoidantly attached leaders tend to minimize the importance of emotional connections, focusing instead on tasks, goals, and outcomes. This can create a leadership style that feels impersonal or distant, leaving team members unsure of where they stand.

Avoidant leaders may struggle with providing feedback, particularly when it involves addressing interpersonal issues. Their discomfort with vulnerability can lead to a reluctance to engage in emotionally charged conversations, whether it's acknowledging a team member's contributions or addressing conflicts. This avoidance may be perceived as indifference, undermining trust and morale within the team.

However, avoidantly attached leaders often excel in high-pressure situations that require quick decision-making and a focus on results. Their ability to remain calm and objective can provide stability during crises, particularly when balanced with efforts to build relational connections. To enhance their effectiveness, avoidant leaders can focus on developing emotional intelligence and practicing small acts of vulnerability, such as expressing appreciation or seeking input from their team. These gestures can help bridge the gap between their task-oriented approach and the relational needs of their employees.

Disorganized attachment presents a unique challenge in leadership, as it combines elements of both anxious and avoidant tendencies. Leaders with this attachment style often exhibit inconsistent or unpredictable behaviors, which can create confusion and tension within their teams. For example, they may alternate between micromanaging and detaching, or between seeking input from their team and dismissing it entirely. This inconsistency is often rooted in internal conflict, as they grapple with a desire for connection and a simultaneous fear of vulnerability.

In high-pressure situations, disorganized leaders may struggle to regulate their emotions, leading to reactive or erratic decision-making. Their unpredictability can make it difficult for team members to establish trust, as they may feel uncertain about how the leader will respond in different scenarios. Additionally, disorganized leaders may have difficulty maintaining clear boundaries, blurring the lines between personal and professional relationships in ways that can create discomfort or misunderstanding.

Despite these challenges, leaders with disorganized attachment styles possess significant potential for growth. Their experiences often give them a heightened sensitivity to relational dynamics, which can be an asset in navigating complex team interactions. With the right support —such as leadership coaching, mentorship, or training in emotional regulation—they can develop greater consistency and self-awareness, enabling them to lead with greater clarity and effectiveness.

The Ripple Effects of Attachment-Informed Leadership

The attachment style of a leader extends far beyond their immediate interactions, shaping the broader culture of their organization. Leaders set the tone for how employees communicate, collaborate, and resolve conflicts, creating either a virtuous cycle of trust and engagement or a negative spiral of mistrust and disengagement. Securely attached leaders are particularly adept at fostering positive organizational cultures, as their behaviors promote emotional safety, respect, and inclusion.

Conversely, insecure attachment styles can introduce relational challenges that ripple through teams and departments. For instance, an anxiously attached leader's need for reassurance may inadvertently create a culture of micromanagement, stifling creativity and autonomy. An avoidantly attached leader's reluctance to engage in relational aspects of work may lead to a lack of cohesion and morale, as employees feel unsupported or undervalued. Disorganized attachment can exacerbate these dynamics, as inconsistent behaviors undermine predictability and trust.

However, attachment-informed leadership practices offer a pathway to address these challenges. By recognizing their own attachment tendencies, leaders can take deliberate steps to create environments that prioritize emotional safety and collaboration. For example, a leader with avoidant tendencies might schedule regular check-ins to build rapport with their team, while an anxious leader might focus on setting clear expectations to reduce overdependence on validation. These small but intentional actions can have a transformative impact, fostering trust and engagement across the organization.

Attachment-informed leadership is not just about individual growth; it is about fostering systemic change within organizations. Leaders who understand the impact of their attachment styles and those of their team members are better equipped to navigate relational dynamics, manage conflicts, and inspire collaboration. This awareness is particularly critical in today's evolving professional landscape, where diverse teams, hybrid work environments, and rapid innovation demand a high level of relational intelligence.

One of the most significant contributions of attachment theory to leadership is its emphasis on emotional safety. Leaders who prioritize emotional safety create environments where employees feel valued, heard, and empowered to take risks. This foundation of trust is essential for fostering innovation, as it encourages individuals to voice new ideas and challenge assumptions without fear of negative repercussions. Securely attached leaders excel in this area, but those with insecure attachment styles can also develop these skills through intentional practice and support.

Organizations can support attachment-informed leadership by providing resources and training that focus on emotional intelligence, communication, and conflict resolution. Leadership development programs that incorporate attachment theory offer practical tools for addressing relational challenges and building stronger connections within teams. These programs also emphasize the importance of self-awareness, helping leaders identify and address their own attachment-related tendencies.

Leadership Styles and Organizational Outcomes

The influence of a leader's attachment style extends beyond individual relationships, shaping the overall performance and resilience of their organization. Teams led by securely attached leaders tend to exhibit higher levels of engagement, trust, and cohesion, creating a positive cycle of productivity and morale. These teams are more adaptable to change, as their foundation of emotional safety enables them to navigate uncertainty with confidence.

In contrast, teams led by insecurely attached leaders may face relational challenges that hinder their effectiveness. For instance, an anxiously attached leader's micromanagement may stifle creativity, while an avoidantly attached leader's emotional detachment can lead to disengagement. Disorganized attachment, with its unpredictability, can create a sense of instability that undermines team cohesion and performance.

However, the integration of attachment-informed practices can mitigate these challenges and enhance organizational outcomes. By fostering a culture of trust, empathy, and collaboration, leaders can create environments where both individuals and teams thrive. These practices not only improve immediate performance but also contribute to long-term organizational success, as employees feel supported and motivated to contribute their best work.

Redefining Leadership Through Attachment Theory

Attachment theory provides a powerful framework for understanding and enhancing leadership. By recognizing the relational patterns that influence their behaviors, leaders can take intentional steps to foster trust, collaboration, and emotional safety within their teams. This chapter has explored the diverse ways in which attachment styles shape leadership, highlighting both the challenges and opportunities they present.

As this book progresses, the insights gained here will be applied to specific aspects of professional life, from conflict resolution and team dynamics to organizational culture. By embracing attachment-informed leadership practices, professionals can create workplaces that are not only more effective but also more humane, paving the way for a future where connection and collaboration are at the heart of success.

Chapter 6: Building Collaborative Relationships

Collaboration is at the heart of organizational success. Whether it involves brainstorming innovative solutions, executing complex projects, or resolving conflicts, the ability to work effectively with others is essential in professional settings. Yet, collaboration is often easier said than done. It requires not only technical skills and shared goals but also a deep understanding of relational dynamics. Attachment theory provides a unique lens for fostering collaborative relationships, emphasizing the importance of trust, emotional safety, and empathy in achieving meaningful cooperation.

Attachment styles significantly influence how individuals approach collaboration. Securely attached individuals tend to engage with confidence and openness, valuing the input of others and contributing constructively to team efforts. Their ability to balance independence with interdependence makes them natural collaborators, as they are comfortable both leading and following. In contrast, insecure attachment styles—whether anxious, avoidant, or disorganized—can introduce challenges that complicate team dynamics. These patterns often manifest in behaviors such as overdependence, withdrawal, or inconsistency, which can hinder trust and cohesion.

Understanding these dynamics is crucial for building effective collaborative relationships. By recognizing the attachment-driven tendencies that shape workplace interactions, professionals can navigate challenges with greater empathy and adaptability. This process begins with establishing a foundation of trust, which serves as the cornerstone of successful collaboration.

Trust: The Foundation of Collaboration

Trust is the invisible thread that binds teams together, enabling individuals to share ideas, take risks, and depend on one another. In the context of attachment theory, trust is deeply influenced by an individual's internal working model of relationships. Securely attached individuals are more likely to approach collaboration with a baseline of trust, assuming that their colleagues will act in good faith. This outlook allows them to engage fully in team efforts, contributing their skills and perspectives without fear of exploitation or rejection.

For those with insecure attachment styles, trust can be more challenging to establish. Anxiously attached individuals may fear being undervalued or excluded, leading them to seek constant reassurance from their teammates. This need for validation can sometimes create tension, as it may be perceived as excessive or demanding. Avoidantly attached individuals, on the other hand, may struggle to trust others' competence or intentions, preferring to rely on their own efforts rather than risk vulnerability. Disorganized attachment introduces further complexity, as these individuals may vacillate between trust and mistrust, creating unpredictability in their relationships.

Building trust within a team requires intentional effort. Clear communication, consistent follow-through, and mutual respect are essential components of trust-building. Leaders play a pivotal role in modeling these behaviors, demonstrating reliability and openness in their interactions. By fostering an environment where trust is valued and reinforced, organizations can create the conditions for meaningful collaboration.

Collaboration extends beyond trust; it requires creating an environment where individuals feel emotionally safe to contribute. Emotional safety allows team members to share ideas, express concerns, and engage in constructive conflict without fear of judgment or retaliation. This sense of safety is critical for fostering innovation and problem-solving, as it encourages individuals to take risks and think creatively.

Attachment theory provides valuable insights into the role of emotional safety in collaboration. Securely attached individuals naturally contribute to emotionally safe environments, as their confidence and openness set a positive tone for team interactions. Their willingness to listen actively, validate others' perspectives, and engage in respectful dialogue creates a ripple effect, encouraging others to do the same.

Insecure attachment styles, however, can pose challenges to emotional safety. Anxiously attached individuals may hesitate to share their ideas, fearing rejection or criticism. Their heightened sensitivity to relational dynamics can make them overly cautious, limiting their contributions to group discussions. Avoidantly attached team members, by contrast, may disengage from collaborative efforts, viewing them as unnecessary or intrusive. Their reluctance to engage emotionally can create a sense of distance, making it harder for the team to build cohesion. Disorganized attachment adds further complexity, as these individuals may oscillate between intense engagement and abrupt withdrawal, creating uncertainty about their intentions.

To foster emotional safety in collaborative relationships, leaders and teams must prioritize empathy and inclusion. This begins with active listening—giving full attention to what others are saying and responding thoughtfully. It also involves creating structured opportunities for dialogue, such as regular team check-ins or brainstorming sessions, where all voices are encouraged and valued. When individuals feel heard and respected, they are more likely to engage fully in collaborative efforts.

Bridging Differences in Collaboration

One of the most significant challenges in building collaborative relationships is navigating differences in attachment styles. These differences can create misalignments in expectations and communication, leading to misunderstandings or conflict. For instance, an anxiously attached employee might perceive an avoidantly attached colleague's preference for autonomy as a lack of interest in collaboration. Similarly, avoidantly attached individuals may feel overwhelmed by an anxious colleague's frequent check-ins or requests for feedback.

Bridging these differences requires a combination of self-awareness and adaptive strategies. Individuals must first recognize their own attachment tendencies and how these influence their approach to collaboration. For example, an anxiously attached team member might work on managing their need for reassurance, focusing instead on building internal confidence. Avoidantly attached individuals, on the other hand, might practice small steps toward vulnerability, such as expressing appreciation for their teammates' efforts or seeking input on a project.

Teams can also benefit from open discussions about collaboration styles and preferences. Encouraging team members to share how they work best—whether they prefer detailed planning or flexible brainstorming, for instance—helps set clear expectations and reduces potential friction. Leaders play a critical role in facilitating these conversations, ensuring that all perspectives are heard and respected.

Effective collaboration is not just about managing individual differences; it is about fostering a shared sense of purpose and connection. Attachment theory emphasizes the importance of relational bonds in creating this sense of unity, highlighting how emotional safety and trust combine to support collective effort. When team members feel connected to one another and aligned toward a common goal, collaboration becomes more intuitive and rewarding.

Building a shared sense of purpose begins with clear and consistent communication. Teams thrive when they understand their objectives, roles, and expectations, as well as how their individual contributions fit into the larger picture. Securely attached individuals naturally excel in creating and sustaining this clarity, as their confidence and openness enable them to articulate goals and navigate challenges effectively. Leaders with secure attachment styles, in particular, are skilled at aligning their teams around a shared vision, fostering motivation and cohesion.

However, insecure attachment styles can complicate the process of creating unity. Anxiously attached individuals may focus too heavily on relational dynamics, becoming preoccupied with gaining approval rather than contributing to the team's objectives. Avoidantly attached team members, by contrast, may resist efforts to build connection, prioritizing their independence over the group's collective goals. Disorganized attachment, with its unpredictability, can further disrupt team alignment, as erratic engagement undermines stability and trust.

To address these challenges, teams must cultivate a culture of mutual respect and accountability. This involves recognizing and valuing the diverse strengths that each member brings to the table, even when attachment-related behaviors create tension. For example, an anxiously attached team member's attentiveness to relational dynamics can enhance group cohesion, while an avoidantly attached colleague's focus on task completion can drive progress. By framing these differences as complementary rather than conflicting, teams can leverage their collective strengths to achieve their goals.

The Role of Feedback in Collaboration

Feedback is a critical component of collaborative relationships, shaping how individuals learn, grow, and contribute to their teams. Attachment theory provides a nuanced perspective on the dynamics of feedback, revealing how different attachment styles influence the way individuals give and receive constructive input.

Securely attached individuals typically approach feedback with openness and curiosity, viewing it as an opportunity for improvement. Their confidence in their own abilities allows them to receive criticism without defensiveness, while their empathy and relational skills make them adept at delivering feedback in a constructive manner. This balanced approach fosters a culture of continuous learning and mutual support within teams.

Insecure attachment styles, however, can create challenges in feedback interactions. Anxiously attached employees may interpret critical feedback as a personal rejection, reacting defensively or seeking excessive reassurance. Avoidantly attached individuals, on the other hand, may dismiss feedback altogether, perceiving it as an intrusion on their autonomy. Disorganized attachment can add further complexity, with individuals alternating between hyper-sensitivity and detachment, making it difficult to predict their responses to feedback.

Leaders play a pivotal role in navigating these dynamics, tailoring their feedback strategies to the needs of their team members. For instance, providing specific, actionable suggestions helps reduce ambiguity for anxiously attached employees, alleviating their fear of rejection. For avoidantly attached individuals, framing feedback in terms of practical benefits rather than relational expectations can make it more palatable. By adapting their approach to the unique needs of their team, leaders can ensure that feedback is both effective and respectful.

Feedback, trust, and emotional safety all converge in one of the most crucial aspects of collaboration: the ability to navigate and resolve conflicts constructively. Conflict is inevitable in any team setting, but how it is managed determines whether it becomes a destructive force or a catalyst for growth. Attachment theory offers valuable insights into the relational patterns that influence conflict resolution, highlighting both challenges and opportunities for fostering collaboration.

Securely attached individuals are typically well-equipped to handle conflicts in a constructive manner. Their ability to regulate their emotions allows them to remain calm and focused during disagreements, while their confidence in relationships enables them to address issues directly and respectfully. These traits make them effective mediators within teams, as they can help de-escalate tensions and guide discussions toward productive outcomes.

Insecure attachment styles, however, can complicate conflict resolution. Anxiously attached individuals may become overly emotional or reactive, interpreting disagreements as threats to their relationships. This heightened sensitivity can escalate minor conflicts into major disputes, creating unnecessary tension within the team. Avoidantly attached individuals, by contrast, may withdraw from conflict altogether, refusing to engage or address underlying issues. While this avoidance may provide temporary relief, it often allows tensions to fester and resurface later in more damaging ways. Disorganized attachment, with its unpredictability, can further disrupt the conflict resolution process, as inconsistent behaviors and mixed signals create confusion and mistrust.

Practical Strategies for Collaborative Conflict Resolution

Addressing conflicts in a way that supports collaboration requires a combination of empathy, communication, and structure. Leaders and team members must approach disagreements with a mindset of curiosity and problem-solving, focusing on understanding each other's perspectives rather than assigning blame. Attachment-informed strategies can help navigate the specific challenges posed by different attachment styles.

For anxiously attached individuals, creating a structured and emotionally supportive environment is key. Encouraging open dialogue while providing clear guidelines for respectful communication helps them feel secure enough to express their concerns without becoming overwhelmed. Avoidantly attached team members may require a different approach, one that respects their need for emotional distance while gently encouraging engagement. Providing opportunities for written input or one-on-one discussions can make conflict resolution more comfortable for these individuals.

For teams dealing with disorganized attachment dynamics, predictability and reassurance are essential. Establishing clear processes for conflict resolution—such as mediated discussions or conflict management workshops—can reduce ambiguity and foster a sense of stability. By creating a safe and structured space for addressing disagreements, teams can build trust and move forward collaboratively.

Collaboration as a Relational Skill

Building collaborative relationships is not simply about achieving shared goals; it is about fostering connections that enhance both individual and collective potential. Attachment theory provides a framework for understanding the relational dynamics that underpin collaboration, offering insights into how trust, emotional safety, and conflict resolution can be nurtured within teams. By recognizing and addressing the attachment-related needs of their colleagues, professionals can create environments where collaboration thrives.

This chapter has explored the practical applications of attachment theory in fostering collaboration, emphasizing the importance of empathy, adaptability, and proactive leadership. As the book progresses, these principles will be further applied to specific challenges in professional settings, from leadership and organizational culture to managing change and fostering inclusion. By embracing these insights, teams and organizations can unlock new levels of connection, creativity, and success.

Chapter 7: Attachment Styles and Leadership Behaviors

Leadership is inherently relational. While strategic vision and decision-making are critical to a leader's role, it is their ability to navigate interpersonal dynamics that often defines their effectiveness. Attachment theory provides a lens through which to understand how leaders' early relational experiences shape their behaviors, influencing how they connect with their teams, handle challenges, and build organizational culture. By exploring the intersection of attachment styles and leadership, this chapter aims to illuminate the hidden drivers behind leadership behaviors and offer strategies for growth.

Attachment styles—secure, anxious, avoidant, and disorganized—manifest in distinct leadership behaviors. These styles influence how leaders approach authority, manage conflict, and foster collaboration. A securely attached leader, for instance, may demonstrate confidence and empathy, creating an environment where employees feel supported and motivated. Conversely, an anxiously attached leader might struggle with delegation or decision-making, seeking reassurance from their team or superiors. Avoidant leaders may prioritize independence over connection, while disorganized leaders may exhibit inconsistent behaviors that create confusion within their teams.

Recognizing these patterns is the first step toward becoming a more effective leader. Attachment styles are not fixed traits; they are tendencies that can be understood, managed, and even transformed through intentional effort. Leaders who cultivate self-awareness and embrace attachment-informed practices can enhance their relational skills, creating stronger connections with their teams and driving organizational success.

Secure Attachment: The Foundation of Relational Leadership

Securely attached leaders bring a unique set of strengths to their roles, grounded in their confidence, empathy, and relational stability. Their internal working models are shaped by early experiences of trust and reliability, enabling them to approach relationships with openness and authenticity. These qualities make them particularly adept at fostering trust and emotional safety within their teams.

One of the defining characteristics of securely attached leaders is their ability to balance authority with approachability. They are comfortable asserting their vision and making decisions, but they also value input from their team members, recognizing that diverse perspectives enhance problem-solving and innovation. This collaborative approach not only strengthens team cohesion but also empowers employees to take ownership of their work.

Secure leaders are also skilled at managing conflict constructively. They view disagreements as opportunities for growth rather than threats to their authority, addressing issues directly and respectfully. Their ability to regulate their emotions under pressure sets a positive example for their team, reinforcing a culture of respect and accountability.

The impact of secure leadership extends beyond individual relationships to shape the broader organizational culture. Teams led by securely attached individuals often exhibit higher levels of trust, engagement, and resilience. These teams are better equipped to navigate challenges and adapt to change, as their foundation of emotional safety provides a buffer against stress and uncertainty.

While secure attachment provides an ideal model for leadership, many leaders operate with behaviors shaped by insecure attachment styles. These styles—anxious, avoidant, and disorganized—reflect patterns of relational dynamics that can present challenges in professional settings. However, understanding these tendencies not only enables growth but also allows leaders to cultivate more effective relationships with their teams.

Anxious attachment often manifests in leadership behaviors that prioritize relational approval over strategic clarity. Leaders with this style may struggle with delegation, fearing that relinquishing control could lead to mistakes or disapproval. Their need for validation might drive them to seek constant feedback, either from their team or their superiors, which can sometimes create tension or a perception of micromanagement. For example, an anxious leader might repeatedly check in on a team project, not out of distrust but as a way to soothe their own insecurities about their performance.

In conflict situations, anxiously attached leaders may find it challenging to maintain emotional regulation. They may overreact to perceived slights or become overly accommodating to restore harmony, even at the expense of the organization's objectives. This overemphasis on relational dynamics can leave teams feeling pressured or uncertain, as the leader's responses may vary based on their emotional state rather than objective considerations.

To grow as leaders, those with anxious tendencies can benefit from focusing on self-regulation and confidence-building practices. Mindfulness exercises, coaching, or seeking feedback from trusted mentors can help them develop a more balanced approach to leadership. By addressing their own insecurities, these leaders can foster a more stable and empowering environment for their teams.

Avoidant Attachment: Leadership from a Distance

Avoidant attachment shapes leadership behaviors in ways that emphasize independence and self-reliance over relational connection. Leaders with this style often prefer to focus on tasks and outcomes, minimizing the emotional or interpersonal aspects of their role. While this pragmatic approach can be an asset in high-pressure situations, it may also create challenges in team dynamics, particularly when emotional support or collaboration is required.

Avoidantly attached leaders may struggle to engage deeply with their teams, maintaining a professional distance that can feel impersonal or aloof. For example, they might avoid addressing interpersonal conflicts directly, hoping the issues will resolve themselves. Their reluctance to engage emotionally can also make it difficult for team members to feel valued or understood, potentially leading to disengagement or low morale.

Feedback is another area where avoidant tendencies can create challenges. These leaders may deliver feedback in a straightforward, no-nonsense manner, prioritizing efficiency over empathy. While this approach can be effective in certain contexts, it may come across as overly critical or dismissive, particularly to team members with more relationally sensitive attachment styles.

Despite these challenges, avoidantly attached leaders bring valuable strengths to their roles, such as a strong focus on goals and the ability to remain calm under pressure. By recognizing their tendencies and working to integrate relational aspects into their leadership style, these individuals can become more balanced and effective. Small steps, such as expressing appreciation for their team's efforts or engaging in one-on-one conversations, can help bridge the gap between their task-oriented approach and the relational needs of their employees.

Disorganized attachment in leadership presents one of the most complex dynamics, as it is marked by inconsistent and often contradictory behaviors. Leaders with this attachment style may vacillate between anxious and avoidant tendencies, creating an unpredictable relational environment for their teams. This inconsistency can undermine trust, as team members struggle to anticipate how the leader will respond in different situations.

Disorganized leaders may exhibit highly engaging and collaborative behaviors one day, followed by abrupt withdrawal or detachment the next. For example, they might initially encourage input from their team on a strategic decision, only to override those contributions later without explanation. This unpredictability is often rooted in the internal conflict that defines disorganized attachment, where a desire for connection clashes with a fear of vulnerability.

In high-pressure situations, disorganized leaders may struggle to regulate their emotions, leading to reactive or erratic decision-making. Their responses can range from over-involvement—where they micromanage or seek constant reassurance—to complete disengagement, leaving their team without clear guidance. These behaviors can create confusion and frustration within the team, eroding morale and cohesion over time.

However, with the right support, leaders with disorganized attachment can develop greater consistency and relational stability. Coaching or mentoring relationships that emphasize trust and predictability can provide these leaders with a model for healthier interactions. Structured routines, clear communication, and tools for emotional regulation—such as mindfulness practices or stress management techniques—can also help them navigate their internal conflicts and foster more reliable leadership behaviors.

Leadership Styles and Organizational Culture

A leader's attachment style extends far beyond their individual interactions, shaping the broader culture of their organization. Securely attached leaders naturally create environments that prioritize trust, respect, and collaboration. Their consistency and emotional safety set the tone for team dynamics, fostering a workplace culture where employees feel valued and empowered to contribute their best work.

Insecure attachment styles, by contrast, can introduce relational challenges that ripple through the organization. Anxiously attached leaders may inadvertently foster a culture of micromanagement, where employees feel over-monitored or pressured to seek constant approval. Avoidantly attached leaders might contribute to a more disengaged or fragmented culture, where emotional connections and team cohesion take a backseat to individual performance. Disorganized attachment can exacerbate these dynamics, creating uncertainty and instability that hinder the organization's ability to function effectively.

Despite these potential challenges, attachment-informed practices provide a pathway to cultivating healthier organizational cultures. Leaders who recognize and address their attachment tendencies can take deliberate steps to model the behaviors they wish to see in their teams. For example, an avoidantly attached leader might make a conscious effort to engage in team-building activities, while an anxious leader might focus on setting clear boundaries and trusting their employees to perform independently. These intentional actions can create a ripple effect, inspiring positive changes throughout the organization.

Attachment-informed leadership is not only about personal growth; it's also about creating an environment where teams and organizations can thrive. Leaders who understand their attachment tendencies—and those of their team members—are better equipped to foster relationships built on trust, emotional safety, and collaboration. This relational awareness is particularly critical in today's professional landscape, where rapid change, diverse teams, and hybrid work environments demand a deeper understanding of interpersonal dynamics.

One of the most powerful aspects of attachment-informed leadership is its potential to build resilience within teams. Leaders who model secure attachment behaviors—such as openness, consistency, and empathy—create a foundation of trust that enables teams to navigate challenges effectively. This resilience is especially important in high-pressure situations, where the ability to rely on one another becomes critical. Securely attached leaders excel in these scenarios, providing the stability and guidance their teams need to succeed.

Insecure attachment styles, while presenting challenges, also offer opportunities for growth and transformation. Leaders with anxious tendencies can harness their relational sensitivity to build deeper connections with their teams, while avoidant leaders can leverage their independence to promote autonomy and initiative. Disorganized leaders, with the right support, can develop the consistency and clarity needed to inspire trust and confidence. By embracing attachment-informed practices, these leaders can move beyond their limitations and cultivate healthier, more effective relationships.

Practical Steps for Attachment-Informed Leadership

To integrate attachment theory into their leadership, professionals must first develop self-awareness. Reflecting on their own relational patterns and how these influence their behaviors is a critical starting point. For example, a leader might ask themselves: "Do I tend to avoid difficult conversations?" or "Am I seeking too much validation from my team?" Identifying these tendencies allows leaders to take intentional steps toward growth.

Leaders can also benefit from seeking feedback from trusted colleagues, mentors, or coaches who can provide an outside perspective on their leadership style. This feedback can help them identify blind spots and develop strategies for addressing them. For instance, a leader with avoidant tendencies might work on engaging more actively with their team, while an anxious leader might focus on delegating responsibilities with confidence.

Organizations can support attachment-informed leadership by providing resources and training that focus on emotional intelligence, communication, and conflict resolution. Leadership development programs that incorporate attachment theory offer practical tools for addressing relational challenges and building stronger connections within teams. These initiatives not only enhance individual leadership but also contribute to a healthier organizational culture.

Transforming Leadership Through Attachment Theory

Attachment theory provides a transformative framework for understanding leadership behaviors and their impact on teams and organizations. By recognizing the relational patterns that shape their approach, leaders can cultivate the self-awareness and skills needed to foster trust, collaboration, and emotional safety. This chapter has explored the diverse ways in which attachment styles influence leadership, highlighting both the challenges and opportunities they present.

As this book progresses, these insights will be applied to other critical aspects of professional life, including conflict resolution, team dynamics, and organizational culture. By embracing attachment-informed leadership practices, professionals can create workplaces that are not only more effective but also more humane, paving the way for a future where connection and collaboration are at the heart of success.

Chapter 8: Becoming an Emotionally Intelligent Leader

Leadership today demands more than technical expertise or strategic thinking—it requires a deep understanding of human behavior and emotions. Emotional intelligence (EI) has emerged as one of the most critical competencies for effective leadership, enabling leaders to build trust, navigate conflicts, and inspire their teams. Grounded in self-awareness, empathy, and interpersonal skills, EI aligns closely with the principles of attachment theory, offering a framework for understanding and improving relational dynamics in the workplace.

Emotional intelligence is often defined as the ability to recognize, understand, and manage one's own emotions while also navigating the emotions of others. Leaders with high EI are better equipped to create environments of trust and emotional safety, where team members feel valued and motivated to contribute. This capacity is particularly relevant in attachment-informed leadership, as it addresses the relational needs and behaviors associated with different attachment styles.

For securely attached leaders, EI enhances their natural strengths, such as openness, empathy, and emotional regulation. These leaders are adept at building connections and fostering collaboration, creating a ripple effect that strengthens team dynamics. However, for leaders with insecure attachment styles, developing EI can be transformative, offering tools to address their relational challenges and grow into more effective and balanced leaders.

The Foundations of Emotional Intelligence in Leadership

The development of emotional intelligence begins with self-awareness—the ability to recognize and understand one's emotions and how they influence behavior. For leaders, self-awareness is particularly critical, as their actions and decisions set the tone for their teams. A leader who is unaware of their own emotional patterns may unintentionally create tension or confusion, undermining trust and morale.

Attachment theory provides valuable insights into the role of self-awareness in leadership. Securely attached leaders are naturally self-aware, as their internal working models are rooted in confidence and trust. They are comfortable reflecting on their emotions and behaviors, allowing them to navigate challenges with clarity and composure. Insecurely attached leaders, by contrast, may struggle with self-awareness, as their relational patterns are often shaped by unconscious fears or defenses. For example, an anxiously attached leader might overanalyze interactions, seeking validation without recognizing the impact of their behavior on their team. An avoidantly attached leader might dismiss their own emotions, focusing solely on tasks and outcomes while neglecting relational dynamics.

Developing self-awareness requires intentional effort, such as reflecting on past experiences, seeking feedback, and practicing mindfulness. Leaders can benefit from keeping a journal to track their emotional responses in different situations, identifying patterns that may influence their behavior. By cultivating self-awareness, they can better understand their attachment tendencies and take proactive steps to manage them.

Once leaders have developed self-awareness, the next critical component of emotional intelligence is self-regulation. Self-regulation refers to the ability to manage emotions constructively, ensuring they do not negatively impact decisions or relationships. For leaders, this skill is particularly important in high-stakes or stressful situations, where their ability to remain calm and composed sets the tone for their teams.

Attachment theory sheds light on the challenges and opportunities of self-regulation for leaders with different attachment styles. Securely attached leaders tend to excel in this area, as their internal working models are built on trust and stability. They can recognize their emotions without being overwhelmed by them, allowing them to respond thoughtfully rather than react impulsively. For instance, a securely attached leader faced with a team conflict might take a moment to process their emotions before facilitating a constructive conversation.

Insecure attachment styles, however, can complicate self-regulation. Anxiously attached leaders may struggle to manage their emotional responses, particularly in situations where they feel criticized or excluded. Their heightened sensitivity to relational dynamics can lead to overreactions or attempts to placate others at their own expense. Avoidantly attached leaders, by contrast, may suppress their emotions entirely, creating an appearance of detachment or indifference. While this strategy may protect them from vulnerability, it can also hinder their ability to engage authentically with their teams.

Disorganized attachment presents additional challenges, as leaders with this style may experience conflicting impulses that make self-regulation particularly difficult. They might oscillate between emotional outbursts and withdrawal, creating uncertainty within their teams. For these leaders, building self-regulation skills is essential for fostering trust and stability.

Practical Strategies for Self-Regulation

Developing self-regulation requires practice and intentionality. Leaders can begin by cultivating mindfulness, which involves paying attention to the present moment without judgment. Mindfulness practices, such as deep breathing, meditation, or journaling, help leaders become more aware of their emotional states and develop the capacity to pause before reacting. For example, a leader who notices feelings of frustration during a tense meeting might take a few deep breaths to calm themselves before addressing the issue.

Another effective strategy is cognitive reframing, which involves changing the way one interprets a situation. An anxiously attached leader who receives critical feedback, for instance, might reframe the experience as an opportunity for growth rather than a sign of inadequacy. Similarly, an avoidantly attached leader who feels uncomfortable discussing emotions might reframe the conversation as a way to strengthen their team rather than as a personal vulnerability.

Seeking support from trusted colleagues, mentors, or coaches can also aid in developing self-regulation. These relationships provide leaders with a safe space to process their emotions, gain perspective, and receive constructive feedback. For leaders with disorganized attachment, structured support systems are particularly valuable, offering consistency and guidance as they work to navigate their internal conflicts.

Empathy is the third pillar of emotional intelligence and arguably the most relationally impactful skill for leaders. Empathy involves understanding and sharing the feelings of others, allowing leaders to connect with their team members on a deeper level. It fosters trust, enhances communication, and creates an environment where employees feel valued and understood. In the context of attachment theory, empathy is particularly significant, as it enables leaders to address the diverse relational needs of their team members based on their attachment styles.

Securely attached leaders are often naturally empathetic, as their internal working models are rooted in trust and connection. They are skilled at recognizing and validating the emotions of others, even in challenging situations. For example, a secure leader might notice a team member's frustration during a project meeting and address it constructively, ensuring the individual feels heard without derailing the discussion. This ability to balance emotional awareness with task-focused objectives sets a strong foundation for effective leadership.

For leaders with insecure attachment styles, developing empathy may require more intentional effort. Anxiously attached leaders, while highly attuned to relational dynamics, may struggle to balance their own emotional needs with those of others. Their desire for validation can sometimes overshadow their ability to fully understand their team members' perspectives. Avoidantly attached leaders, by contrast, may find it challenging to engage emotionally, as they tend to prioritize tasks over relationships. Their discomfort with vulnerability can make them appear distant or unapproachable, even when they care deeply about their team's success.

Disorganized leaders may face additional hurdles, as their inconsistent behaviors can create confusion or mistrust within their teams. Building empathy for these leaders involves cultivating stability in their relationships and developing greater self-awareness of their own emotional states. Over time, these efforts can enhance their ability to connect with others and foster a sense of trust and understanding.

Building Empathy as a Leadership Skill

Leaders can develop empathy through active listening, a skill that involves giving full attention to what others are saying without interrupting or jumping to conclusions. Active listening not only improves understanding but also signals to team members that their perspectives are valued. For example, a leader might paraphrase a team member's concerns to ensure clarity, such as, "If I understand correctly, you're feeling uncertain about the timeline for this project. Is that right?" This approach encourages open dialogue and reinforces emotional safety.

Another key strategy is practicing perspective-taking, which involves imagining how others might feel in a given situation. For instance, an avoidantly attached leader who prefers minimal communication might reflect on how a lack of feedback could impact an anxiously attached team member. By considering the emotional experience of their team, leaders can adapt their behaviors to better meet their needs.

Leaders can also foster empathy by seeking diverse viewpoints and encouraging team members to share their experiences. This practice not only enhances relational understanding but also promotes inclusivity and innovation. For leaders with avoidant or disorganized attachment tendencies, participating in team-building activities or facilitated discussions can help bridge emotional gaps and strengthen connections.

The final component of emotional intelligence is social skills—the ability to navigate and influence interpersonal relationships effectively. For leaders, strong social skills translate into the capacity to inspire, guide, and unify their teams. This involves not only managing individual relationships but also fostering collaboration and cohesion across the organization. Attachment theory provides a valuable lens for understanding how leaders can develop and apply these skills, addressing the relational dynamics that shape workplace interactions.

Securely attached leaders often excel in social skills, as their confidence and emotional regulation enable them to engage with others in meaningful and constructive ways. They are skilled at resolving conflicts, motivating their teams, and building consensus, all while maintaining a focus on shared goals. These leaders approach social interactions with authenticity and empathy, creating an environment where employees feel valued and supported.

Insecure attachment styles, however, can present challenges to the development of social skills. Anxiously attached leaders may become overly focused on pleasing others, leading to behaviors that prioritize harmony over effectiveness. For instance, they might avoid making difficult decisions to avoid disappointing their team, inadvertently creating confusion or delays. Avoidantly attached leaders, on the other hand, may struggle to engage relationally, preferring to focus on tasks rather than the interpersonal aspects of their role. This detachment can hinder their ability to build rapport or address team dynamics.

Disorganized attachment adds a layer of unpredictability, as leaders with this style may alternate between intense engagement and withdrawal. Their inconsistent behaviors can create uncertainty within their teams, making it difficult to establish stable and productive relationships. Developing social skills for these leaders requires a focus on consistency, communication, and relational stability.

Practical Strategies for Enhancing Social Skills

Leaders can strengthen their social skills by practicing effective communication, which involves both clarity and empathy. This includes articulating expectations clearly, providing constructive feedback, and actively engaging in dialogue with team members. For example, a leader might use a collaborative approach to problem-solving, encouraging input from their team while guiding the discussion toward actionable outcomes.

Conflict resolution is another critical area for developing social skills. Leaders must approach disagreements with a mindset of curiosity and collaboration, focusing on understanding different perspectives rather than assigning blame. Attachment theory offers specific strategies for navigating conflict based on relational dynamics. For instance, a leader working with an anxiously attached team member might provide reassurance while addressing the issue directly, ensuring the individual feels supported without avoiding the problem.

Building relational networks is also essential for enhancing social skills. Leaders can benefit from developing relationships across different levels of the organization, fostering connections that promote trust and collaboration. Participating in mentorship programs, attending team events, or engaging in cross-departmental initiatives are all effective ways to strengthen social ties and expand relational influence.

Emotional Intelligence as a Transformative Leadership Tool

Emotional intelligence is more than a set of skills—it is a mindset that empowers leaders to navigate the complexities of professional relationships with empathy, awareness, and intentionality. By integrating the principles of attachment theory into their approach, leaders can deepen their understanding of relational dynamics and foster environments where trust, collaboration, and emotional safety thrive.

This chapter has explored the four pillars of emotional intelligence—self-awareness, self-regulation, empathy, and social skills—emphasizing their relevance in attachment-informed leadership. As we continue through this book, these insights will be applied to other critical aspects of professional life, including conflict resolution, team dynamics, and organizational culture. By embracing emotional intelligence as a core leadership competency, professionals can create workplaces that are not only more effective but also more human.

Chapter 9: Understanding Conflict Through the Lens of Attachment

Conflict is an inevitable aspect of professional life. While disagreements and differing perspectives can drive innovation and growth, unresolved or poorly managed conflicts often lead to tension, disengagement, and reduced productivity. To navigate these challenges effectively, it is essential to understand the underlying dynamics that shape how individuals perceive and respond to conflict. Attachment theory offers a unique lens for examining the roots of workplace conflict, revealing how relational patterns and emotional needs influence behavior.

Attachment styles—secure, anxious, avoidant, and disorganized—play a significant role in how individuals approach conflict. These styles, shaped by early experiences of connection and trust, influence not only how people interpret the intentions of others but also how they express their own concerns. For example, securely attached individuals are more likely to address conflicts directly and constructively, viewing disagreements as opportunities for growth. Insecurely attached individuals, however, may experience heightened emotional reactivity or avoid confrontation altogether, creating additional challenges for resolution.

Recognizing these patterns is the first step in addressing conflict through an attachment-informed approach. By understanding the relational needs and fears that drive behaviors, leaders and teams can adopt strategies that foster empathy, reduce defensiveness, and promote constructive dialogue.

Attachment Styles and Their Impact on Conflict

Secure attachment provides a strong foundation for navigating conflict effectively. Individuals with this style are confident in their relationships and comfortable expressing their needs and concerns.

They approach disagreements with curiosity and openness, focusing on finding solutions rather than assigning blame. Securely attached individuals are also skilled at regulating their emotions during conflict, which helps them remain calm and composed even in tense situations.

Insecure attachment styles, by contrast, introduce challenges that can complicate conflict resolution. Anxiously attached individuals often view conflict as a threat to their relationships, leading them to react emotionally or seek excessive reassurance. For instance, they might become overly apologetic or escalate minor issues in an attempt to gain validation. These behaviors, while rooted in a desire for connection, can create additional tension within the team.

Avoidantly attached individuals take a different approach, often minimizing or dismissing conflicts altogether. Their discomfort with vulnerability leads them to avoid addressing issues directly, hoping that the problem will resolve itself over time. While this strategy may provide temporary relief, it often allows underlying tensions to persist, potentially escalating into more significant disputes.

Disorganized attachment combines elements of both anxious and avoidant tendencies, creating a complex and often unpredictable approach to conflict. Individuals with this style may alternate between seeking connection and withdrawing, leaving their colleagues uncertain about how to engage with them. This inconsistency can exacerbate misunderstandings and make it challenging to resolve conflicts constructively.

The ways in which individuals perceive and respond to conflict are deeply rooted in their attachment experiences, shaping their relational patterns and emotional regulation strategies. In professional settings, these tendencies can manifest in ways that either mitigate or exacerbate tensions. To effectively address conflict, it is essential to recognize how these underlying dynamics influence behaviors and interactions.

Anxiously attached individuals often approach conflict with heightened emotional sensitivity. Their internal working models are shaped by a fear of rejection or abandonment, which can lead them to interpret disagreements as personal attacks. This heightened vigilance may result in defensive behaviors, such as overexplaining their position, seeking constant reassurance, or escalating the issue to gain attention. For instance, an anxiously attached employee might repeatedly revisit a disagreement with a colleague, not out of malice but out of a need to feel understood and valued.

While their emotional engagement can bring attention to unresolved issues, it can also overwhelm their colleagues, who may perceive their behavior as disproportionate to the situation. Leaders working with anxiously attached team members can address these challenges by providing consistent reassurance and creating structured opportunities for dialogue. For example, scheduled check-ins can help anxiously attached individuals feel heard while preventing their concerns from dominating team dynamics.

Avoidantly attached individuals, by contrast, tend to disengage from conflict, viewing it as an unnecessary or uncomfortable distraction. Their internal working models emphasize self-reliance, leading them to minimize relational tensions or avoid addressing them altogether. This avoidance can create a perception of indifference, as colleagues may feel unsupported or dismissed. For example, an avoidantly attached manager might downplay a team member's concerns during a meeting, leaving the issue unresolved and contributing to frustration within the team.

Leaders can help avoidantly attached individuals engage more effectively in conflict resolution by framing disagreements as opportunities for growth rather than threats to autonomy. Providing clear, task-focused objectives can also reduce the emotional burden of conflict, making it easier for these individuals to participate constructively.

Disorganized Attachment and Conflict Dynamics

Disorganized attachment introduces a particularly complex dynamic to workplace conflict, as it combines the heightened emotional reactivity of anxious attachment with the withdrawal tendencies of avoidant attachment. Individuals with disorganized attachment often experience internal conflict, torn between seeking connection and fearing vulnerability. This internal struggle can lead to inconsistent and unpredictable behaviors during disagreements.

For example, a disorganized team member might initially confront a colleague about an issue, only to withdraw or disengage before the conflict is resolved. Alternatively, they might alternate between intense emotional expression and complete detachment, leaving their colleagues uncertain about how to respond. These patterns can create confusion and tension within teams, as the lack of consistency undermines trust and predictability.

Addressing conflict with disorganized individuals requires a focus on emotional safety and stability. Leaders can create a supportive environment by establishing clear expectations and providing consistent feedback. Structured conflict resolution processes, such as mediation or facilitated discussions, can also help reduce ambiguity and foster a sense of control for individuals with disorganized attachment tendencies.

Conflict often escalates when underlying relational needs and fears are left unaddressed. Attachment theory highlights how these dynamics play out in professional settings, where unresolved tensions can strain relationships and hinder collaboration. Recognizing these patterns is key to transforming conflict from a source of division into an opportunity for growth and connection.

One of the most common triggers for conflict in the workplace is misaligned expectations. These misalignments are often amplified by attachment-related tendencies. For instance, anxiously attached individuals may expect frequent feedback or reassurance from their colleagues, interpreting a lack of communication as a sign of disinterest or rejection. Conversely, avoidantly attached individuals may expect others to respect their independence and limit emotional engagement, viewing attempts at connection as intrusive or unnecessary.

These conflicting expectations can create a cycle of misunderstanding and frustration. For example, an anxiously attached employee might perceive their avoidantly attached manager's concise feedback as dismissive, prompting them to seek further clarification or validation. The manager, in turn, might view the employee's behavior as overly dependent, leading them to withdraw further. Without intervention, this dynamic can escalate, resulting in strained relationships and reduced productivity.

Leaders play a critical role in breaking these cycles by fostering a culture of open communication and mutual understanding. Encouraging team members to articulate their needs and preferences—while also considering those of others—helps align expectations and reduce potential conflicts. For example, a leader might facilitate a team discussion where individuals share their preferred communication styles, creating a foundation for empathy and collaboration.

The Role of Emotional Regulation in Conflict Resolution

Emotional regulation is a cornerstone of effective conflict resolution, as it enables individuals to manage their responses and approach disagreements constructively. Attachment styles significantly influence emotional regulation, shaping how people process and express their emotions during conflict.

Securely attached individuals are typically skilled at regulating their emotions, as their internal working models provide a sense of stability and confidence. This allows them to approach conflicts with a calm and solution-focused mindset, even in high-pressure situations. For example, a securely attached leader might address a tense team disagreement by acknowledging everyone's perspectives and guiding the discussion toward a compromise.

Insecure attachment styles, however, can pose challenges to emotional regulation. Anxiously attached individuals may become overwhelmed by their emotions, reacting impulsively or defensively to perceived threats. Avoidantly attached individuals, by contrast, may suppress their emotions entirely, avoiding confrontation but allowing unresolved tensions to build over time. Disorganized attachment adds further complexity, as individuals with this style may alternate between intense emotional expression and withdrawal, creating unpredictability in their responses.

Building emotional regulation skills is essential for navigating these challenges. Mindfulness practices, such as deep breathing or grounding exercises, can help individuals remain present and composed during conflicts. Leaders can model these behaviors for their teams, demonstrating how to approach disagreements with empathy and clarity. Additionally, providing training on emotional intelligence and conflict management equips employees with the tools to regulate their emotions and engage constructively in challenging conversations.

Resolving conflict in the workplace requires more than addressing immediate disagreements; it involves creating an environment where trust, emotional safety, and mutual respect can flourish. Attachment theory provides a powerful framework for understanding how to achieve this, offering insights into the relational patterns that influence both the origins and outcomes of conflict.

One of the most effective ways to resolve conflict is through attachment-informed dialogue. This approach emphasizes empathy, active listening, and a focus on underlying needs rather than surface-level issues. For example, a leader navigating a disagreement between an anxiously attached employee and an avoidantly attached colleague might facilitate a conversation that acknowledges both parties' perspectives. By validating the anxiously attached individual's desire for connection and the avoidantly attached individual's need for independence, the leader can guide the discussion toward a solution that respects both relational needs.

Structured conflict resolution processes are particularly valuable for teams with diverse attachment styles. Techniques such as mediation, facilitated discussions, or even anonymous feedback channels provide safe and predictable spaces for addressing disagreements. These processes reduce the ambiguity that often triggers insecurity in anxiously or disorganized attached individuals while encouraging avoidantly attached individuals to engage without feeling overwhelmed. Leaders can enhance these efforts by establishing clear norms for respectful communication, ensuring that all team members feel heard and valued.

Fostering a Culture of Constructive Conflict

A key aspect of managing conflict through an attachment lens is fostering a culture that views disagreements as opportunities for growth rather than threats to relationships. Securely attached individuals naturally model this mindset, approaching conflicts with curiosity and openness. However, for teams with a mix of attachment styles, creating this culture requires intentional effort and leadership.

Leaders can set the tone by normalizing conflict as a part of team dynamics and providing the tools to navigate it effectively. This might involve hosting workshops on conflict resolution, encouraging team members to reflect on their own conflict styles, or incorporating attachment theory into leadership development programs. For instance, a team-building exercise might explore how different attachment styles approach disagreements, helping individuals develop empathy for one another's perspectives.

Celebrating successful conflict resolution also reinforces a positive approach to disagreements. When teams see that addressing conflicts constructively leads to stronger relationships and better outcomes, they are more likely to engage openly in future challenges. Over time, this mindset transforms conflict from a source of division into a catalyst for connection and collaboration.

Conflict as an Opportunity for Growth

Understanding conflict through the lens of attachment theory provides a deeper appreciation for the relational dynamics that shape workplace interactions. By recognizing the influence of attachment styles on conflict behaviors, professionals can approach disagreements with greater empathy and effectiveness. This chapter has explored the roots of conflict in attachment patterns, highlighting practical strategies for resolution and growth.

As we continue through this book, the principles of attachment theory will be applied to other critical aspects of professional life, including team dynamics, leadership, and organizational culture. By embracing these insights, individuals and organizations can transform conflict into an opportunity for innovation, connection, and mutual understanding.

Chapter 10: Strategies for Managing and Resolving Workplace Conflicts

Conflict resolution in the workplace is both an art and a science. While every disagreement has unique elements, effective strategies for resolving conflicts often share common principles: empathy, communication, and a focus on finding mutually beneficial outcomes. Attachment theory enriches this process by offering insights into the relational dynamics that influence how individuals perceive and respond to conflict. By understanding these dynamics, professionals can tailor their conflict resolution approaches to meet the needs of diverse attachment styles.

Attachment-informed conflict resolution begins with recognizing that disagreements are not merely about tasks or outcomes; they often reflect deeper relational needs and fears. For example, an anxiously attached employee might interpret a colleague's critical feedback as a personal rejection, while an avoidantly attached team member might disengage entirely to avoid confrontation. Addressing these underlying concerns is essential for achieving meaningful and lasting resolutions.

One of the first steps in managing workplace conflicts is creating an environment of emotional safety. When individuals feel secure and respected, they are more likely to engage openly and constructively in the resolution process. Leaders play a critical role in fostering this environment by modeling calm and empathetic behaviors, setting clear expectations for respectful communication, and ensuring that all voices are heard.

Building a Foundation for Conflict Resolution

Effective conflict resolution relies on a foundation of trust and mutual respect. Without these elements, even minor disagreements can escalate into significant challenges. Attachment theory highlights the importance of relational trust in navigating conflicts, as individuals' attachment styles often shape their willingness to engage in difficult conversations.

Securely attached individuals are naturally inclined to address conflicts constructively, as their confidence in relationships allows them to approach disagreements with openness and curiosity. They are skilled at expressing their concerns without assigning blame, focusing on collaborative problem-solving rather than defensiveness. For example, a securely attached leader might begin a conflict resolution discussion by acknowledging the perspectives of all parties involved, setting a tone of mutual respect and understanding.

Insecure attachment styles, however, can complicate the process. Anxiously attached individuals may struggle to regulate their emotions during conflicts, reacting defensively or seeking excessive reassurance. Avoidantly attached individuals, by contrast, may avoid addressing conflicts altogether, hoping the issue will resolve itself over time. Disorganized attachment adds further complexity, as individuals with this style may exhibit unpredictable behaviors that create confusion or tension.

To address these challenges, conflict resolution strategies must be tailored to the relational needs of each individual. For instance, providing consistent reassurance and structured opportunities for dialogue can help anxiously attached employees feel more secure. For avoidantly attached individuals, emphasizing the practical benefits of resolving the conflict—such as improved workflow or clearer expectations—can encourage engagement without overwhelming them emotionally.

Once a foundation of trust and emotional safety is established, the next step in conflict resolution is fostering open and constructive communication. Attachment theory provides valuable insights into how communication patterns are shaped by attachment styles, highlighting the importance of empathy and adaptability in addressing disagreements effectively.

Securely attached individuals excel in conflict resolution discussions, as they are comfortable expressing their needs and listening to others without becoming defensive. Their balanced communication style helps create an atmosphere of respect and collaboration, making it easier to reach mutually beneficial outcomes. For example, a securely attached team member might address a conflict by calmly articulating their concerns and inviting their colleague to share their perspective, setting the stage for a productive dialogue.

Insecure attachment styles, however, can lead to communication challenges that complicate the resolution process. Anxiously attached individuals may become overly emotional or reactive, struggling to articulate their concerns without assigning blame. Their heightened sensitivity to relational dynamics can make them misinterpret neutral statements as criticism, escalating the conflict unnecessarily. Avoidantly attached individuals, by contrast, may withhold their thoughts or feelings altogether, creating a communication gap that hinders resolution. Disorganized attachment adds further complexity, as individuals with this style may alternate between emotional outbursts and withdrawal, leaving others uncertain about how to engage with them.

Empathy and Active Listening in Conflict Resolution

One of the most effective tools for managing these dynamics is empathy—the ability to understand and validate others' emotions and perspectives. Empathy not only fosters trust but also reduces defensiveness, making it easier to address the underlying issues driving the conflict. For instance, a leader facilitating a conflict resolution discussion might begin by acknowledging the emotions of each party involved, such as saying, "I understand that this situation has been frustrating for both of you. Let's work together to find a solution that feels fair and constructive."

Active listening is another critical skill in conflict resolution, particularly when navigating attachment-related challenges. Active listening involves giving full attention to the speaker, reflecting back their statements for clarity, and responding thoughtfully. For example, when working with an anxiously attached employee, a manager might say, "I hear that you're feeling unheard in team meetings. Can you share more about what changes would help you feel more included?" This approach not only validates the individual's concerns but also encourages them to engage constructively in finding solutions.

For avoidantly attached individuals, active listening can help bridge the gap between their preference for autonomy and the relational needs of the team. By creating a low-pressure environment for dialogue—such as one-on-one discussions rather than group meetings—leaders can encourage avoidantly attached employees to share their perspectives without feeling overwhelmed.

While effective communication is central to resolving conflicts, addressing the emotional undercurrents that often accompany disagreements is equally important. Emotional regulation plays a pivotal role in ensuring that conflicts are managed constructively rather than escalating into more significant issues. Attachment theory highlights how different attachment styles influence emotional responses during conflict, offering guidance on how to navigate these dynamics.

Anxiously attached individuals often experience heightened emotional responses in conflict situations. Their fear of rejection or disconnection can amplify their reactions, leading to behaviors such as over-apologizing, becoming overly defensive, or escalating the issue in an attempt to secure reassurance. For example, an anxiously attached team member might interpret a colleague's disagreement as a personal slight, prompting them to respond with excessive justifications or appeals for validation. These behaviors, while stemming from a need for connection, can sometimes overwhelm or frustrate others.

Avoidantly attached individuals, by contrast, tend to suppress their emotions during conflicts, often appearing detached or indifferent. This avoidance may be a coping mechanism to protect themselves from vulnerability, but it can also create a perception of disengagement or lack of concern. For instance, an avoidantly attached leader might downplay a team member's frustration, responding with a brief acknowledgment rather than engaging in a deeper conversation. While this approach may provide temporary relief for the leader, it often leaves the underlying issues unresolved.

Disorganized attachment introduces a unique complexity to emotional regulation, as individuals with this style may oscillate between intense emotional expression and withdrawal. This inconsistency can create confusion within teams, as colleagues may struggle to anticipate or respond to the disorganized individual's behavior. For example, a disorganized leader might initially react to a conflict with anger or frustration, only to disengage entirely when confronted with the need for resolution.

Strategies for Supporting Emotional Regulation

Leaders and team members can foster constructive conflict resolution by promoting emotional regulation techniques tailored to different attachment styles. Mindfulness practices, such as deep breathing or grounding exercises, can help anxiously attached individuals manage their heightened emotional responses. For instance, a leader might encourage a team member to take a moment to reflect before responding during a tense discussion, providing the space needed to process their emotions constructively.

For avoidantly attached individuals, creating a structured and task-focused approach to conflict resolution can make the process feel less emotionally charged. Framing the discussion around practical outcomes—such as improving team efficiency or clarifying roles—helps avoidantly attached employees engage without feeling overwhelmed by relational dynamics. Additionally, providing opportunities for written input or one-on-one conversations can reduce the pressure of group interactions, encouraging more open communication.

For individuals with disorganized attachment, consistency and predictability are key to fostering emotional regulation. Leaders can create structured processes for addressing conflicts, such as setting clear agendas for resolution meetings or outlining specific steps for follow-up. Offering reassurance and maintaining a calm, nonjudgmental tone helps reduce the unpredictability that often exacerbates disorganized attachment tendencies.

Resolving workplace conflicts requires not only addressing immediate disagreements but also fostering a culture where differences are valued, and misunderstandings are seen as opportunities for growth. Attachment theory offers a relational perspective that emphasizes trust, empathy, and emotional safety as foundational elements of effective conflict resolution. By integrating these principles into organizational practices, leaders and teams can build environments where conflicts are navigated constructively.

A critical component of conflict resolution is establishing clear and predictable processes for addressing disagreements. Structured approaches—such as mediation, facilitated discussions, or formalized feedback sessions—provide a safe space for individuals to express their concerns and work toward resolution. These processes are particularly valuable in teams with diverse attachment styles, as they reduce ambiguity and create a sense of stability. For example, a leader facilitating a conflict resolution discussion might outline the steps in advance, such as defining the issue, exploring perspectives, and agreeing on actionable solutions. This structure helps individuals with insecure attachment styles feel more secure and engaged.

Another important strategy is reframing conflict as a natural and necessary part of collaboration. Securely attached leaders often model this mindset, viewing disagreements as opportunities to strengthen relationships and improve processes. For instance, a leader might say, "Conflict isn't about winning or losing—it's about understanding each other better so we can work more effectively as a team." This perspective shifts the focus from blame to growth, creating an environment where team members feel encouraged to engage openly.

Conflict Resolution as a Relational Skill

Developing conflict resolution skills is a relational process that benefits from ongoing practice and reflection. Leaders can enhance their effectiveness by seeking feedback from their teams, reflecting on past conflicts, and identifying areas for improvement. For example, a leader might ask their team, "What worked well during our last conflict resolution discussion, and what could we do differently next time?" This openness not only fosters trust but also signals a commitment to continuous growth.

Attachment-informed training programs can further support conflict resolution efforts by equipping leaders and employees with the tools to navigate relational dynamics. Workshops on emotional intelligence, active listening, and communication styles help teams understand the impact of attachment patterns on conflict and provide practical strategies for addressing them. These programs also emphasize the importance of self-awareness, encouraging individuals to reflect on their own tendencies and how they influence their interactions.

Building a Culture of Constructive Conflict

Conflict is an inevitable aspect of professional life, but it does not have to be a source of division. By applying the principles of attachment theory, organizations can transform conflict into a relational skill that strengthens teams and fosters innovation. This chapter has explored practical strategies for managing and resolving workplace conflicts, emphasizing the importance of trust, empathy, and emotional regulation.

As this book continues, these insights will be applied to broader aspects of professional life, including organizational culture and the creation of emotionally safe workplaces. By embracing attachment-informed practices, leaders and teams can build environments where conflict is not feared but embraced as an opportunity for connection and growth.

Chapter 11: Creating Inclusive and Emotionally Safe Work Environments

In today's diverse and dynamic professional landscape, creating inclusive and emotionally safe work environments is both a moral imperative and a strategic advantage. Employees who feel valued and supported are more engaged, productive, and innovative, contributing to the overall success of their organizations. Attachment theory provides a powerful framework for understanding the relational dynamics that underpin inclusivity and emotional safety, offering insights into how these principles can be integrated into workplace culture.

At its core, emotional safety refers to an environment where individuals feel secure enough to express themselves without fear of judgment, rejection, or retaliation. This sense of safety is essential for fostering open communication, collaboration, and trust. Attachment styles play a significant role in shaping how employees experience emotional safety at work. Securely attached individuals are more likely to feel confident and included in their teams, while those with insecure attachment styles may struggle to navigate relational dynamics, making them more vulnerable to feelings of exclusion or anxiety.

Inclusivity goes hand in hand with emotional safety, as it ensures that all employees—regardless of their backgrounds, identities, or attachment tendencies—feel valued and respected. An inclusive workplace recognizes and celebrates diversity, creating spaces where individuals can bring their whole selves to work. Attachment theory enriches this understanding by highlighting how relational needs and patterns influence employees' sense of belonging and engagement.

The Role of Leadership in Fostering Inclusion and Safety

Leaders play a critical role in shaping the culture of their organizations, setting the tone for how employees interact, collaborate, and resolve conflicts. Securely attached leaders are particularly well-suited to fostering inclusive and emotionally safe environments, as their confidence, empathy, and relational stability enable them to model the behaviors they wish to see in their teams. These leaders create spaces where employees feel heard, valued, and supported, encouraging open dialogue and mutual respect.

For example, a securely attached leader might begin team meetings by inviting input from all members, ensuring that everyone has an opportunity to contribute. They might also address interpersonal tensions proactively, using their emotional intelligence to mediate conflicts and reinforce trust. These behaviors not only enhance team dynamics but also set a standard for inclusivity and safety that permeates the organization.

Insecure attachment styles, however, can pose challenges to fostering inclusion and safety. Anxiously attached leaders may focus excessively on maintaining harmony, avoiding difficult conversations that could disrupt relationships. Avoidantly attached leaders, by contrast, may struggle to engage deeply with their teams, prioritizing tasks over relational connection. Disorganized attachment adds further complexity, as inconsistent behaviors can create uncertainty and tension within teams.

Recognizing these tendencies is the first step for leaders seeking to create more inclusive and emotionally safe environments. By cultivating self-awareness and developing attachment-informed practices, leaders can address their relational challenges and foster cultures that prioritize connection, trust, and respect.

Creating emotionally safe and inclusive environments requires more than leadership intentions; it demands intentional strategies and structures that address the relational needs of all employees. Attachment theory provides a lens for understanding how individuals with different attachment styles experience workplace dynamics, highlighting the importance of tailoring approaches to foster belonging and engagement across diverse teams.

For anxiously attached employees, emotional safety hinges on consistent communication and reassurance. These individuals are highly attuned to relational dynamics and may interpret ambiguous interactions as signals of rejection or exclusion. For example, an anxiously attached team member might feel slighted if their contributions in a meeting are not explicitly acknowledged, leading to feelings of insecurity or disengagement. Leaders can support these employees by providing regular feedback, recognizing their efforts, and creating structured opportunities for dialogue. By offering clarity and validation, organizations can help anxiously attached individuals feel secure and valued.

Avoidantly attached employees, by contrast, may prioritize autonomy and independence, viewing relational engagement as unnecessary or uncomfortable. While these traits can be strengths in roles requiring self-direction, they may also hinder collaboration and inclusion. For instance, an avoidantly attached team member might resist participating in team-building activities or view open discussions about emotions as intrusive. Leaders can create a balance by respecting these employees' need for independence while encouraging gradual engagement in relational aspects of work. Framing collaboration as a practical tool for achieving goals, rather than an emotional requirement, can help avoidantly attached individuals feel more comfortable participating.

Disorganized attachment presents unique challenges in fostering emotional safety, as individuals with this style may exhibit inconsistent behaviors that create uncertainty within teams. These employees may alternate between seeking connection and withdrawing, making it difficult for colleagues to build stable relationships with them. Leaders can support disorganized employees by establishing clear expectations and routines, providing consistent feedback, and offering reassurance. Structured mentorship or coaching programs can also help these individuals develop greater relational stability and confidence.

The Importance of Representation in Inclusion

Inclusion is not only about creating safe spaces for individual engagement; it also involves ensuring that employees see themselves reflected in their organization's leadership and decision-making processes. Representation plays a crucial role in fostering a sense of belonging, as it signals to employees that their identities and perspectives are valued.

Attachment theory underscores the relational nature of representation, emphasizing the importance of role models in shaping individuals' sense of security and belonging. For employees with insecure attachment styles, the presence of relatable leaders or colleagues can provide a source of reassurance and connection, reducing feelings of isolation or alienation. For instance, a junior employee from an underrepresented background might feel more confident and engaged if they see leaders who share their experiences and values.

Organizations can promote representation by prioritizing diversity in hiring, mentorship, and leadership development programs. These efforts should go beyond tokenism, focusing instead on creating meaningful opportunities for individuals from diverse backgrounds to contribute and thrive. Attachment-informed practices, such as fostering emotional safety and addressing relational dynamics, enhance these initiatives by ensuring that employees feel supported and included at every level of the organization.

Building emotionally safe and inclusive environments requires organizations to go beyond addressing individual needs and focus on cultivating a culture that prioritizes relational well-being. Attachment theory offers practical insights into how this can be achieved by emphasizing trust, empathy, and connection as foundational elements of workplace culture. When employees experience these qualities consistently, they are more likely to engage fully, collaborate effectively, and contribute to organizational success.

One of the most significant contributors to emotional safety is predictability. Attachment theory highlights the importance of consistent and reliable interactions in fostering secure relationships. In the workplace, predictability can take many forms, from clear communication of expectations to consistent application of policies and procedures. For example, a manager who regularly provides feedback and follows through on commitments helps create a sense of stability that is particularly valuable for anxiously or disorganized attached employees.

Empathy also plays a crucial role in fostering emotional safety and inclusion. Empathetic leaders and colleagues create spaces where employees feel understood and respected, even during disagreements or challenges. Attachment theory underscores the relational impact of empathy, as it helps bridge differences in attachment styles and fosters trust across teams. For instance, a leader who recognizes that an avoidantly attached employee may need time to process feedback before responding can adapt their approach to ensure that the individual feels respected and supported.

Establishing Shared Values and Norms

A strong organizational culture is built on shared values and norms that guide behaviors and interactions. Attachment-informed practices emphasize the importance of relational norms that prioritize connection, respect, and inclusivity. These norms create a framework for emotional safety, ensuring that all employees—regardless of their attachment styles—feel supported and valued.

One way to establish shared values is through collaborative vision-setting processes that involve input from employees at all levels. For example, an organization might host workshops or focus groups to identify the core principles that define its culture, such as mutual respect, open communication, or commitment to diversity. These principles then serve as a foundation for decision-making and conflict resolution, reinforcing a culture of inclusion.

Organizations can also reinforce these values through training and professional development programs. Workshops on emotional intelligence, communication styles, and attachment-informed leadership help employees and leaders alike understand the relational dynamics that influence workplace interactions. These programs not only enhance individual skills but also promote a collective commitment to fostering emotional safety and inclusion.

Creating an inclusive and emotionally safe work environment extends beyond interpersonal relationships—it requires systemic practices and policies that prioritize well-being and equity. Attachment theory provides a framework for designing these systems, emphasizing the importance of stability, fairness, and relational connection in fostering a culture where all employees can thrive. By aligning organizational policies with attachment-informed principles, companies can institutionalize inclusion and emotional safety, making these values an integral part of their identity.

One of the most impactful ways to achieve this alignment is through onboarding and training programs that introduce employees to the organization's commitment to emotional safety and inclusion from the outset. For example, new hire orientations can include sessions on the company's attachment-informed approach to leadership, communication, and conflict resolution. These sessions not only set expectations but also signal to employees that their relational well-being is a priority.

Regularly assessing and addressing barriers to inclusion is another critical component of fostering emotional safety. Organizations can conduct surveys or focus groups to identify areas where employees feel excluded or unsupported, using this feedback to implement targeted interventions. For instance, if employees from certain backgrounds report feeling undervalued, leadership can respond by creating mentorship programs, resource groups, or career development opportunities tailored to their needs.

The Role of Leadership in Sustaining Culture

Leaders are the stewards of organizational culture, and their behaviors significantly influence whether inclusion and emotional safety are consistently upheld. Attachment-informed leadership practices emphasize the relational aspects of culture-building, such as modeling empathy, maintaining transparency, and addressing conflicts constructively. Leaders who embody these values create a ripple effect, inspiring their teams to do the same.

For example, a leader who actively listens to their team's concerns and provides thoughtful responses reinforces a culture of respect and emotional safety. Similarly, a leader who takes responsibility for their mistakes demonstrates humility and accountability, setting a powerful example for their team. These behaviors not only strengthen relationships but also build trust across the organization.

Sustaining an inclusive and emotionally safe culture also requires ongoing education and self-reflection. Leaders can benefit from regular training on attachment theory and emotional intelligence, as well as opportunities to receive feedback from their teams. By committing to their own growth, leaders can continuously improve their ability to support their employees and foster a culture of connection and collaboration.

Toward a More Inclusive and Relational Workplace

Creating inclusive and emotionally safe work environments is not a one-time effort but an ongoing process that requires commitment, empathy, and adaptability. By applying the principles of attachment theory, organizations can design cultures that prioritize trust, respect, and relational well-being, ensuring that all employees feel valued and supported.

This chapter has explored how attachment-informed practices can guide the development of inclusive cultures, emphasizing the importance of leadership, shared values, and systemic policies. As we approach the final chapter of this book, these insights will be synthesized to explore the future of workplace relationships and the role of attachment theory in shaping professional life.

Chapter 12: Measuring and Enhancing Emotional Safety in the Workplace

Emotional safety is both an intangible and essential element of a healthy workplace. It fosters trust, collaboration, and innovation, enabling employees to engage fully and perform at their best. While the benefits of emotional safety are widely recognized, assessing and enhancing it requires intentionality and a deep understanding of relational dynamics. Attachment theory offers a unique framework for this effort, emphasizing the role of secure relationships in creating environments where employees feel valued, respected, and empowered.

Measuring emotional safety begins with identifying the specific factors that contribute to a sense of security within the workplace. These factors often include trust in leadership, the quality of interpersonal relationships, the perceived fairness of organizational policies, and the ability to voice concerns without fear of reprisal. Attachment theory highlights the relational nature of these factors, suggesting that emotional safety is not merely the absence of conflict but the presence of connection and support.

Organizations can assess emotional safety through a combination of qualitative and quantitative methods. Employee surveys, focus groups, and one-on-one interviews provide valuable insights into how employees perceive their work environment and relationships. For example, a survey might ask employees to rate statements such as "I feel comfortable sharing my ideas with my manager" or "My team values my contributions." These responses help identify areas where emotional safety is strong and where it may need improvement.

The Relational Context of Emotional Safety

Attachment theory underscores the importance of relational dynamics in shaping employees' experiences of emotional safety. Securely attached individuals are more likely to perceive their workplace as emotionally safe, as their internal working models predispose them to trust and connect with others. They are comfortable expressing their needs, seeking feedback, and engaging in collaboration, all of which contribute to a positive work environment.

Insecure attachment styles, however, can influence how employees experience and contribute to emotional safety. Anxiously attached individuals may be more sensitive to perceived slights or exclusions, requiring additional reassurance and validation to feel secure. Avoidantly attached individuals, by contrast, may disengage from relational aspects of work, viewing emotional safety as irrelevant or unnecessary. Disorganized attachment adds further complexity, as inconsistent behaviors can create uncertainty and tension within teams.

Understanding these attachment-related tendencies is essential for designing effective interventions to enhance emotional safety. For example, leaders might implement initiatives that provide additional support for anxiously attached employees, such as regular check-ins or clear feedback processes. For avoidantly attached individuals, creating opportunities for low-pressure engagement—such as asynchronous brainstorming sessions or one-on-one meetings—can encourage participation without overwhelming them emotionally.

To enhance emotional safety effectively, organizations must adopt strategies that address the diverse relational needs of their workforce. Attachment theory highlights the importance of tailoring interventions to the attachment styles present within a team, ensuring that all employees feel supported and included. This requires a multi-layered approach that integrates individual, team, and organizational initiatives.

At the individual level, fostering emotional safety begins with self-awareness. Employees and leaders alike benefit from reflecting on their relational patterns and how these influence their interactions at work. For instance, a leader with avoidant tendencies might recognize that their preference for autonomy sometimes comes across as disengagement, prompting them to take small steps toward more relational engagement. Similarly, an anxiously attached team member might work on developing internal confidence, reducing their reliance on external validation.

Team-level initiatives play a crucial role in creating emotionally safe environments, as they provide opportunities for collaboration, trust-building, and conflict resolution. Attachment theory emphasizes the importance of predictability and consistency in fostering secure relationships, suggesting that structured team practices can enhance emotional safety. For example, regular team check-ins, collaborative goal-setting sessions, and facilitated discussions about communication styles help establish norms of openness and respect. These practices not only reduce ambiguity but also create spaces where employees feel empowered to contribute and share their perspectives.

Assessing Emotional Safety in Teams

Measuring emotional safety at the team level involves evaluating both relational dynamics and operational practices. Surveys and assessments designed to capture team members' perceptions of trust, inclusion, and communication are valuable tools for identifying strengths and areas for improvement. For example, a survey might include questions such as "Do you feel comfortable providing feedback to your team members?" or "Does your team handle disagreements constructively?"

Qualitative methods, such as focus groups or facilitated team discussions, provide deeper insights into the relational dynamics influencing emotional safety. These conversations can uncover subtle patterns of exclusion, miscommunication, or mistrust that may not surface in quantitative data. For instance, a focus group might reveal that certain team members feel hesitant to voice their ideas during meetings due to perceived hierarchies or dominant personalities. Addressing these issues requires a thoughtful approach that balances individual accountability with collective responsibility.

Attachment-informed strategies can guide these efforts by emphasizing empathy and inclusivity. For example, a leader might implement a practice where every team member has equal time to speak during meetings, ensuring that all voices are heard. This not only fosters emotional safety but also reinforces the team's commitment to collaboration and mutual respect.

Emotional safety extends beyond individual relationships and team dynamics; it requires systemic organizational support. Attachment theory offers a framework for understanding how policies, practices, and leadership behaviors collectively shape the emotional climate of a workplace. Organizations that prioritize emotional safety embed these principles into their structures, ensuring that all employees, regardless of their attachment styles, feel valued and supported.

A critical component of organizational emotional safety is fairness and transparency. Attachment theory underscores the importance of predictability in fostering secure relationships, and this principle applies to organizational policies as well. When employees trust that rules and procedures are applied consistently, they are more likely to feel emotionally safe. For example, transparent performance evaluation processes reduce the ambiguity that can trigger anxiety or mistrust, particularly for anxiously attached employees. Similarly, clear pathways for career advancement ensure that all employees have equal opportunities for growth, fostering a sense of inclusion.

Organizational leaders play a pivotal role in reinforcing these values through their actions and communication. Securely attached leaders naturally model behaviors that promote emotional safety, such as consistency, empathy, and active engagement. Insecurely attached leaders, however, may require targeted support to align their behaviors with these principles. Leadership development programs that incorporate attachment-informed practices can help leaders build the self-awareness and relational skills needed to foster emotional safety within their teams.

Leveraging Technology to Enhance Emotional Safety

Technology offers innovative tools for measuring and improving emotional safety in the workplace. Employee engagement platforms, for instance, provide real-time feedback on organizational climate, helping leaders identify and address areas where emotional safety may be lacking. Attachment-informed survey tools can capture nuanced data about relational dynamics, such as employees' perceptions of trust, inclusion, and communication within their teams.

For example, an attachment-informed engagement survey might include statements like, "I feel supported by my manager when I face challenges at work," or "Our team has a clear and respectful process for resolving conflicts." These insights allow organizations to tailor their interventions to address specific needs, such as providing additional training for leaders or introducing new communication protocols.

Digital tools can also facilitate emotional safety by creating channels for anonymous feedback or asynchronous communication. These options are particularly valuable for avoidantly attached employees, who may feel more comfortable sharing their thoughts in written formats rather than face-to-face discussions. Similarly, anxiously attached employees benefit from structured communication platforms that provide consistent opportunities for feedback and dialogue.

Sustaining emotional safety in the workplace requires a long-term commitment to continuous improvement. Attachment theory emphasizes the dynamic nature of relationships, highlighting that emotional safety is not a fixed state but a process that evolves over time. Organizations must regularly assess their practices, gather feedback, and adapt to the changing needs of their employees to maintain a secure and inclusive environment.

One effective way to ensure ongoing progress is through the integration of emotional safety metrics into organizational performance reviews. These metrics, informed by attachment principles, can assess how well teams and leaders are fostering trust, inclusion, and collaboration. For example, leadership evaluations might include questions such as, "Does this leader demonstrate empathy and active listening?" or "How effectively does this leader address relational challenges within their team?" Incorporating these measures into performance reviews reinforces the organization's commitment to relational well-being and holds leaders accountable for their role in fostering emotional safety.

Regular training and development programs also play a crucial role in sustaining emotional safety. Workshops on attachment-informed leadership, emotional intelligence, and conflict resolution equip employees and leaders with the tools to navigate relational dynamics effectively. These programs should be iterative, incorporating feedback from participants to ensure they remain relevant and impactful.

The Business Case for Emotional Safety

Investing in emotional safety is not only a moral imperative but also a strategic advantage. Research consistently shows that emotionally safe workplaces experience higher levels of employee engagement, productivity, and retention. When employees feel secure and supported, they are more likely to take risks, innovate, and contribute their best work. These benefits extend beyond individual performance, enhancing team cohesion and organizational resilience.

Attachment theory provides a unique perspective on the mechanisms behind these outcomes, emphasizing the importance of trust and connection in driving motivation and collaboration. For example, a team that values emotional safety is better equipped to handle challenges and adapt to change, as their foundation of trust enables them to navigate uncertainty with confidence. This adaptability is particularly critical in today's fast-paced and dynamic professional landscape, where organizations must continually evolve to remain competitive.

Institutionalizing Emotional Safety

Measuring and enhancing emotional safety is an ongoing journey that requires commitment, intentionality, and a deep understanding of relational dynamics. By applying the principles of attachment theory, organizations can create environments where employees feel valued, supported, and empowered to succeed. This chapter has explored the tools and strategies for assessing and fostering emotional safety, emphasizing the importance of leadership, systemic practices, and technological innovation.

As this book concludes, the insights gained from attachment theory provide a roadmap for transforming workplace relationships and cultures. By prioritizing emotional safety and inclusion, organizations can unlock the full potential of their teams, fostering both individual and collective success.

Conclusion: Attachment Theory and the Future of Work

As we approach the conclusion of this exploration into attachment theory's relevance in the professional world, it becomes clear that the insights derived from this framework are more than theoretical—they are transformative. The workplace is fundamentally relational, a tapestry woven from the interactions, behaviors, and emotional landscapes of the people within it. Attachment theory serves as a powerful lens to examine these dynamics, providing a roadmap for understanding, improving, and reimagining the environments where we work, lead, and grow.

The professional world is experiencing a paradigm shift. Traditional models of workplace relationships, often transactional and hierarchical, are giving way to approaches that prioritize connection, trust, and collaboration. The rise of remote work, hybrid teams, and increasingly diverse organizational cultures has only amplified the need for relational awareness and emotional intelligence. In this context, attachment theory provides not just answers but essential tools to address these emerging challenges.

Attachment theory reminds us that relationships are at the core of every professional interaction. Whether it's the bond between leaders and their teams, the dynamics within workgroups, or the culture of an entire organization, the principles of secure, trusting connections underpin the success of all these elements. Securely attached individuals and cultures foster environments where innovation thrives, challenges are navigated with resilience, and relationships become sources of strength rather than stress. Conversely, insecure attachment tendencies—whether expressed through avoidance, anxiety, or inconsistency—can lead to misunderstandings, conflict, and disengagement. Recognizing these patterns is the first step toward transforming them.

The Broader Implications of Emotional Safety

Emotional safety is one of the most profound contributions of attachment theory to the professional domain. In the absence of fear or judgment, individuals are free to express themselves, take risks, and innovate. Emotional safety is the bedrock of psychological safety, a concept increasingly recognized as critical for team performance and organizational success. Attachment theory deepens our understanding of emotional safety by highlighting its roots in early relational experiences and demonstrating how these patterns influence professional interactions.

In today's rapidly evolving workplaces, emotional safety takes on new dimensions. Remote work and digital communication, while offering flexibility and efficiency, often lack the relational nuances of face-to-face interactions. These changes demand a renewed focus on fostering connection and trust, even when physical proximity is limited. Attachment theory equips leaders and teams with strategies to bridge these gaps, emphasizing empathy, active listening, and consistent communication as tools to maintain relational security in virtual settings.

Moreover, emotional safety is not just about individual well-being—it is a driver of organizational performance. Teams that operate with a foundation of trust and respect are better equipped to navigate challenges, adapt to change, and achieve shared goals. Leaders who model attachment-informed practices—such as providing consistent feedback, addressing conflicts constructively, and recognizing the relational needs of their teams—set the tone for a culture where emotional safety becomes the norm.

While emotional safety is a cornerstone of effective workplace dynamics, its impact extends far beyond individual relationships. At an organizational level, emotional safety fosters a culture where collaboration and inclusion flourish, enabling teams to harness the full potential of their diversity. Attachment theory provides a framework for understanding how these cultural elements develop and offers strategies for embedding them into the fabric of organizational life.

Diversity and inclusion, for example, are not simply goals to be achieved but ongoing processes that require relational awareness and intentionality. Attachment-informed practices emphasize the importance of recognizing and addressing the relational needs of all employees, particularly those who may feel marginalized or excluded. For instance, anxiously attached individuals may need additional reassurance to feel valued, while avoidantly attached employees may benefit from initiatives that respect their independence while encouraging connection. By tailoring approaches to these diverse needs, organizations can create environments where everyone feels empowered to contribute.

Inclusion is not just about representation; it's about creating spaces where employees feel a sense of belonging and engagement. Attachment theory highlights the relational underpinnings of belonging, emphasizing the importance of trust, mutual respect, and emotional connection. Organizations that prioritize these elements through their policies, leadership practices, and day-to-day interactions create cultures where employees are not just present but fully invested in their work and relationships.

The Transformative Power of Relational Leadership

Leadership, as explored throughout this book, is one of the most significant drivers of workplace dynamics. Attachment theory underscores the relational nature of leadership, offering insights into how leaders' attachment styles influence their behaviors, decisions, and impact on their teams. Securely attached leaders, with their balance of confidence, empathy, and consistency, naturally foster environments of trust and emotional safety. Their ability to regulate their emotions and engage constructively with others sets the tone for a healthy and collaborative workplace culture.

Insecure attachment styles, while presenting challenges, also offer opportunities for growth and transformation. Leaders with anxious tendencies can harness their relational sensitivity to build deeper connections with their teams, provided they work on developing self-regulation and confidence. Avoidantly attached leaders, on the other hand, can leverage their focus on autonomy and efficiency by integrating relational practices that enhance engagement without overwhelming their natural tendencies. Disorganized attachment requires more intentional support, but with structured guidance and consistent feedback, leaders with this style can develop the stability and predictability needed to inspire trust.

The transformative potential of attachment-informed leadership lies in its ability to address the relational complexities of professional life. By recognizing and addressing their own attachment tendencies, leaders not only enhance their effectiveness but also model behaviors that ripple through their organizations. Teams led by attachment-informed leaders are more likely to exhibit higher levels of trust, resilience, and collaboration, creating a foundation for sustained success.

As workplaces become increasingly diverse and interconnected, the relational insights offered by attachment theory take on even greater significance. Modern organizations are not static entities; they are dynamic systems influenced by global trends, technological advancements, and shifting cultural expectations. Attachment theory provides a stable foundation for navigating these changes, emphasizing the enduring importance of trust, empathy, and connection in professional relationships.

One of the most profound applications of attachment theory is its ability to guide organizations through periods of uncertainty and change. Change often disrupts established relational patterns, heightening anxiety and uncertainty among employees. Attachment theory highlights how individuals with different attachment styles respond to change and offers strategies for managing these responses constructively. For instance, securely attached individuals tend to view change as an opportunity for growth, approaching it with curiosity and resilience. In contrast, anxiously attached employees may need additional reassurance during transitions, while avoidantly attached employees might require clear, task-focused communication to remain engaged.

Leaders play a pivotal role in guiding their teams through change, modeling attachment-informed behaviors that foster stability and trust. Transparent communication, consistent decision-making, and empathetic engagement are critical during periods of upheaval. For example, a leader navigating an organizational restructuring might hold regular updates to address employees' concerns, ensuring that all team members feel informed and supported. By prioritizing relational well-being during change, leaders can mitigate its disruptive effects and strengthen their teams' capacity for adaptation.

Attachment Theory in Remote and Hybrid Workplaces

The rise of remote and hybrid work has reshaped professional relationships, challenging traditional notions of connection and collaboration. Attachment theory offers valuable insights into how these changes impact relational dynamics, highlighting the need for intentional efforts to maintain emotional safety and trust in virtual settings.

Remote work often limits the spontaneous interactions that foster connection, such as casual conversations or impromptu check-ins. This can be particularly challenging for anxiously attached individuals, who may feel isolated or disconnected without regular face-to-face engagement. Leaders can address these challenges by implementing structured opportunities for virtual connection, such as scheduled one-on-one meetings or team-building activities conducted online. These practices provide anxiously attached employees with the reassurance and engagement they need to feel secure.

For avoidantly attached employees, the independence of remote work may align with their preferences, but it can also exacerbate disengagement from relational aspects of their roles. Leaders can encourage these employees to participate in collaborative projects or virtual discussions, framing these activities as opportunities to achieve shared goals rather than emotional obligations.

Hybrid work models, which combine in-person and remote elements, present unique opportunities and challenges for fostering relational security. Attachment-informed practices can guide organizations in designing hybrid environments that balance flexibility with connection. For instance, organizations might designate specific days for in-person collaboration, creating opportunities for relationship-building while maintaining the autonomy of remote work.

The insights provided by attachment theory extend beyond individual relationships and team dynamics to address broader questions about the future of work. As organizations grapple with evolving professional landscapes, attachment-informed practices offer a guiding framework for building workplaces that are not only effective but also deeply human. These practices emphasize the importance of relational well-being as a driver of innovation, resilience, and long-term success.

One of the most exciting frontiers for attachment theory is its application to global and cross-cultural collaboration. In an increasingly interconnected world, professionals must navigate differences in language, culture, and social norms while maintaining trust and emotional safety. Attachment theory highlights the universal need for connection and belonging, providing a shared foundation for fostering understanding across diverse contexts. For instance, a leader managing a multicultural team might use attachment-informed strategies to address relational tensions, ensuring that all team members feel valued and included despite their differences.

Technological advancements also present opportunities to integrate attachment principles into the workplace. Artificial intelligence and digital tools can be designed to support emotional safety by facilitating clear communication, providing consistent feedback, and offering platforms for anonymous input. For example, AI-powered coaching programs can help leaders develop emotional intelligence, while digital collaboration tools can create spaces for team members to connect and share ideas securely.

A Vision for Relational Workplaces

Attachment theory offers more than a framework for understanding relationships; it presents a vision for reimagining the workplace itself. In a relational workplace, trust is the foundation of every interaction, and connection is prioritized alongside productivity. These environments recognize the inherent value of human relationships, fostering cultures where employees feel seen, heard, and empowered to contribute their best work.

Leaders play a central role in bringing this vision to life. By modeling attachment-informed behaviors—such as empathy, consistency, and openness—they create a ripple effect that influences their teams and organizations. Securely attached leaders set the standard for what relational workplaces can achieve, demonstrating that emotional safety and inclusivity are not just ideals but practical tools for driving success.

Organizations that embrace this vision will be better equipped to navigate the complexities of the modern professional landscape. Whether adapting to new technologies, responding to societal shifts, or addressing global challenges, attachment-informed workplaces provide a stable foundation for growth and innovation. These environments are not only more resilient but also more humane, reflecting the values of connection and collaboration that underpin attachment theory.

A Call to Action

As this book comes to a close, the principles of attachment theory remain an open invitation to transform the way we work and lead. Whether you are a leader striving to build trust within your team, an employee seeking to navigate workplace relationships, or an organizational architect shaping the future of your company, your actions have the power to create meaningful change.

By embracing attachment-informed practices, you can foster workplaces where emotional safety, inclusivity, and connection are at the heart of success. These environments not only support individual well-being but also unlock the collective potential of teams and organizations. As we look to the future, the relational insights of attachment theory provide a roadmap for building workplaces that are not only effective but also profoundly human.

The future of work is relational. Together, we can create environments where trust and connection thrive, ensuring that the professional world becomes a place of growth, resilience, and shared success.

Case Study 1: Conflict Between Leadership and an Anxiously Attached Employee

Professional Context:
In a small, family-owned travel agency, the team consists of five members: the manager, two senior travel agents, a recently hired employee, and an administrative assistant. The atmosphere in the agency is generally informal, but the workload intensifies during peak holiday seasons.

The manager, Julia, adopts a transformational leadership style and emphasizes innovation and adaptability. She focuses on improving internal processes, including the implementation of new booking technologies and expanding the range of services offered. However, Julia has an avoidant attachment style, which means she tends to focus more on tasks and less on emotional connections, often preferring independence and autonomy for herself and her team. While she is a competent leader, Julia struggles with emotionally charged situations and is less likely to provide frequent, supportive feedback to her team members.

The Conflict:
Pierre, one of the senior travel agents, has an anxious attachment style. He seeks validation and approval in his work and has a heightened fear of failure and rejection. During the implementation of a new booking system, Pierre encountered technical issues and made mistakes that led to some dissatisfaction from clients. Although he informed Julia about his concerns, she offered minimal feedback, focusing primarily on the technical aspects of the mistakes without offering emotional reassurance. Julia's responses were task-oriented and did not acknowledge the effort Pierre had put into his work.

This lack of emotional support heightened Pierre's anxiety. He began to feel rejected and unsupported, perceiving Julia's indifference as a sign of disapproval. As a result, Pierre became increasingly desperate for validation and began highlighting the issues with the system repeatedly. Julia, in turn, felt overwhelmed by these requests for validation and withdrew further, leaving Pierre feeling even more insecure and unsupported.

The Impact on the Team:
The conflict between Julia and Pierre quickly affected the atmosphere within the agency. The other two senior agents noticed the growing tension and became uncomfortable in their work. The team's communication deteriorated, leading to a breakdown in collaboration. Even the administrative assistant, who was responsible for processing client files and supporting the team, began feeling the effects of the strained relationships, which disrupted her ability to work efficiently.

The emotional distance between Julia and Pierre created a toxic dynamic where both felt misunderstood and disengaged. Pierre's attempts to seek validation went unanswered, while Julia's avoidance of emotional topics led to further frustration. As a result, the agency's performance began to suffer due to decreased productivity, lower morale, and heightened stress levels.

Points of Analysis:

1. **Pierre's anxious attachment style** is central to the conflict. His constant need for validation and emotional reassurance was not met by Julia, which increased his feelings of anxiety and led him to seek attention in ways that escalated the conflict.

2. **Julia's avoidant attachment style** contributed to a lack of emotional support for Pierre. Her tendency to focus solely on task-related issues, without addressing the emotional needs of her team, reinforced Pierre's insecurity and rejection fears.

3. **The lack of open communication and emotional support** between the two parties created a misunderstanding and distrust, which further escalated the conflict.

4. **The impact on the team:** The conflict between Julia and Pierre negatively affected the entire team, creating a more tense and less collaborative work environment. The emotional climate became stressful, and productivity declined as a result.

Possible Solutions:

- **Julia's self-awareness and attachment work:** Julia could benefit from becoming more aware of her avoidant attachment style and how it impacts her leadership approach. Learning to recognize the emotional needs of her team, particularly for employees like Pierre, could help her provide more support and create a healthier, more inclusive work environment.
- **Support for Pierre:** Pierre could benefit from mentoring or coaching to help him manage his anxiety and gain more self-confidence in his work. This would allow him to better handle feedback without becoming overwhelmed.
- **Improving communication:** Regular check-ins with the team, where both task-related and emotional aspects are addressed, could help prevent conflicts from escalating. Open communication about emotional needs would foster better understanding and collaboration within the team.

Case Study 2: Tension Between a Team Leader and an Avoidantly Attached Employee

Professional Context:
In a large marketing firm in London, the team consists of ten employees who work in various roles, including content creation, strategy, and client management. The team has a strong culture of collaboration, with frequent meetings to discuss ongoing projects and brainstorm ideas. The team leader, Tom, is well-respected for his expertise and his ability to drive results. However, Tom struggles with providing emotional support to his team, as he is highly focused on achieving objectives and maintaining high productivity.

One of Tom's team members, Sarah, has an avoidant attachment style. Sarah is a highly competent strategist, but she prefers to work independently and tends to withdraw from team discussions when emotions or personal issues are involved. She is known for her ability to focus intensely on her tasks, delivering quality work on time. However, Sarah often appears disengaged in meetings and tends to avoid any conversation that veers toward interpersonal dynamics or team-building activities.

The Conflict:
Recently, the team has been under pressure to deliver a major marketing campaign for a key client. Tom has been pushing the team hard, holding multiple meetings and providing constant updates to the client. However, during these sessions, Tom noticed that Sarah was becoming increasingly withdrawn. At first, he assumed she was simply focused on her work, but as the project progressed, her withdrawal became more apparent.

Tom, who values open communication and collaboration, began to perceive Sarah's behavior as a lack of commitment or interest in the project. He started pushing her more during meetings, asking for her input more frequently and even calling her out for not participating as actively as the rest of the team. Sarah, feeling uncomfortable and overwhelmed by the attention, started to withdraw even further, avoiding group discussions and becoming more distant. This created tension between them, as Tom interpreted her withdrawal as resistance or disengagement, while Sarah saw Tom's increasing pressure as intrusive and disrespectful of her boundaries.

The Impact on the Team:
The tension between Tom and Sarah began to affect the overall dynamics of the team. Other team members noticed Sarah's withdrawal and began questioning whether she was still fully engaged in the project. This uncertainty led to some awkwardness during meetings, as some members were unsure how to interact with Sarah or whether they should step in to help her. Tom's increasing frustration with Sarah also affected his interactions with the rest of the team, as he became more focused on trying to "fix" Sarah's behavior rather than collaborating with her on the project.

Sarah's performance remained strong, but her emotional withdrawal affected the morale of the team. The team was becoming increasingly divided, with some members supporting Sarah's need for space and others questioning her commitment. The growing tension between Sarah and Tom began to undermine the overall cohesiveness of the team.

Points of Analysis:

1. **Sarah's avoidant attachment style** plays a significant role in the conflict. Her preference for independence and emotional distance led her to withdraw from the team and avoid engaging in the collaborative aspects of the project.

2. **Tom's leadership approach**, focused on productivity and results, created a mismatch with Sarah's emotional needs. His attempt to engage Sarah by increasing pressure rather than providing space for her to work autonomously exacerbated the situation.

3. **Miscommunication and misunderstanding** are central to this conflict. Tom's inability to recognize Sarah's need for emotional space, and Sarah's discomfort with the increasing pressure to engage, led to a breakdown in communication and trust.
4. **The impact on the team:** The tension between Tom and Sarah affected the overall atmosphere, creating division and uncertainty. The lack of emotional support for Sarah and Tom's escalating demands compromised the team's cohesion and collaboration.

Possible Solutions:

- **Tom's self-awareness and adaptability:** Tom could benefit from understanding the attachment dynamics at play and learning how to adapt his leadership style to accommodate employees with avoidant attachment styles. By providing Sarah with more autonomy and reducing pressure, Tom could create a more supportive environment for her to thrive in.
- **Supporting Sarah's emotional needs:** Sarah might benefit from more structured feedback and one-on-one meetings where she feels heard without being overwhelmed. Giving her the opportunity to express her concerns privately, rather than in large meetings, could help her engage more comfortably with the team.
- **Improving team communication:** The team could benefit from fostering an open environment where different communication styles are respected. Creating a culture of understanding regarding attachment styles and relational needs could improve overall collaboration and reduce tension.

Case Study 3: Disagreement Between a Senior Manager and a Disorganized-Attached Employee

Professional Context:
In a mid-sized software development company in the United States, the team is composed of developers, product managers, and customer support agents. The company has a fast-paced, high-pressure environment, with frequent product releases and tight deadlines. The senior manager, Michael, has a reputation for being a results-driven leader who is highly focused on meeting deadlines and achieving targets. He is known for his efficiency, but he struggles with offering emotional support or creating a space for open communication.

One of his employees, Jacob, works in the customer support team. Jacob is a talented and resourceful employee, but he struggles with emotional regulation and often exhibits erratic behaviors in stressful situations. Jacob has a disorganized attachment style, characterized by inconsistent responses to relational cues. He sometimes seeks attention and validation, but other times he withdraws, creating confusion and tension within the team.

The Conflict:
Jacob has been under significant pressure to meet high expectations for customer support during a crucial product launch. He was assigned to handle technical inquiries from clients, which was a new and challenging responsibility for him. During one of the meetings with Michael, Jacob made a mistake in providing information to a key client. Michael, frustrated by the error, reprimanded Jacob in front of the team for not being more careful. Jacob, feeling both embarrassed and threatened, responded by becoming defensive, trying to explain the situation in a way that sounded like an excuse.

Michael, seeing this as a lack of accountability, became even more frustrated and reprimanded Jacob more harshly. This only made Jacob retreat further, withdrawing from the group and distancing himself from his colleagues. Jacob's response was not just emotional withdrawal, but also an outburst later that day in which he accused Michael of not understanding the pressures he was facing. The confrontation, though brief, disrupted the team's focus and led to a breakdown in communication between Michael and Jacob. This dynamic created confusion among the other employees, as they did not know whether the conflict was resolved or if further tension would escalate.

The Impact on the Team:
The conflict had a significant effect on the team's dynamics. Other team members began to avoid Jacob, unsure of how to approach him after the emotional outburst. Some saw his behavior as an overreaction, while others understood it as a reflection of the stress he was under. The ambiguity of Jacob's attachment style made it difficult for his colleagues to interpret his reactions, leading to discomfort and unease in the workplace.

Meanwhile, Michael became more focused on results and less empathetic toward Jacob's needs, interpreting Jacob's defensiveness as a personal flaw rather than recognizing it as a manifestation of deeper emotional stress. The lack of resolution between Michael and Jacob made it difficult for the rest of the team to regain their focus, as they were unsure whether there would be future conflicts or how they could support Jacob moving forward.

Points of Analysis:

1. **Jacob's disorganized attachment style** is central to the conflict. His unpredictable reactions—oscillating between seeking attention and withdrawing—created confusion and tension. Disorganized attachment often manifests in erratic responses, especially under stress, making it difficult for others to understand and respond appropriately.

2. **Michael's leadership style**, focused primarily on achieving results, lacks the emotional intelligence needed to manage

employees with disorganized attachment. His harsh reprimands and lack of emotional support exacerbated Jacob's anxiety and defensive behaviors, leading to a breakdown in communication.

3. **Misinterpretation and lack of emotional safety** were key drivers of this conflict. Michael's failure to recognize Jacob's emotional triggers, combined with Jacob's unpredictable responses, created an environment of tension and misunderstanding. Both parties were unable to address the issue constructively, leading to emotional escalation.

4. **The impact on the team:** The conflict disrupted the team's workflow and led to confusion about how to interact with Jacob. The lack of clear resolution and the emotional tension created an uncomfortable working environment for the rest of the team.

Possible Solutions:

- **Michael's self-awareness and emotional regulation:** Michael could benefit from attachment-informed leadership training that would help him recognize how attachment styles influence employee behavior. By adjusting his communication style and offering more empathetic responses, he could create a more emotionally safe environment for Jacob and the team.
- **Supporting Jacob's emotional needs:** Jacob may benefit from mentoring or coaching that helps him manage his emotional responses and build emotional resilience. Providing Jacob with a structured environment where he feels safe to express his concerns could help him feel more secure and engaged.
- **Creating a culture of emotional safety:** The team could benefit from clearer communication protocols that prioritize emotional safety, allowing employees to address conflict in a healthy and constructive manner. Regular team meetings

focused on both task-related and emotional concerns would ensure that issues are addressed early on and prevent future misunderstandings.

Case Study 4: Tension Between a Young Manager and a Highly Independent Employee

Professional Context:
In a startup based in New York, the team of 15 employees is focused on building an innovative mobile application for small businesses. The company has a dynamic, fast-paced environment where creativity, autonomy, and collaboration are highly valued. The team includes a young manager, Olivia, who was promoted to her position within a year of joining the company. Olivia has been praised for her ambition and drive but struggles with managing interpersonal relationships due to her inexperience and need for control.

On the other hand, Tom, one of the senior developers, has been with the company since its inception. Tom is highly skilled and self-reliant, known for his technical expertise. He has a dismissive-avoidant attachment style, preferring to work independently and avoiding emotional discussions. Tom is known for his strong opinions and reluctance to engage in group activities that he views as unnecessary or inefficient. While he is deeply committed to his work, Tom's need for autonomy and discomfort with authority often put him at odds with Olivia, whose leadership style is more directive.

The Conflict:
The conflict between Olivia and Tom began when Olivia introduced a new project management system aimed at increasing transparency and collaboration within the team. Olivia, being a young manager, was keen to establish clear roles and expectations, but Tom resisted using the new system, preferring his own methods and working without detailed oversight. When Olivia insisted that the team adopt the new system for all project tasks, Tom became increasingly frustrated. He viewed the system as micromanaging and unnecessary, feeling that it undermined his expertise and independence.

Olivia, in turn, interpreted Tom's resistance as a lack of commitment to the team's goals and a refusal to adapt to company changes. She attempted to address the issue in team meetings, but Tom's avoidance of confrontation made it difficult to engage him in a productive discussion. Instead of addressing his concerns directly, Tom began to withdraw even more from the group, opting to work on his tasks in isolation. Olivia's frustration grew, and she began to question Tom's dedication to the team's success.

The conflict escalated when Olivia gave Tom a formal performance review, highlighting his lack of participation in team activities and his unwillingness to adapt to new systems. Tom felt personally attacked and became defensive, stating that his methods had worked in the past and that Olivia was not qualified to judge his work. Olivia, feeling undermined and frustrated by his lack of cooperation, became more directive and less empathetic toward Tom's needs, further escalating the tension between them.

The Impact on the Team:
The tension between Olivia and Tom quickly affected the rest of the team. Other employees became aware of the growing friction, and some of them began to take sides, with a few supporting Olivia's attempts to implement the new systems and others sympathizing with Tom's desire for independence. The division among the team led to a decrease in morale, as employees felt uncomfortable navigating the rift between their manager and a senior team member. The team's collaborative spirit, which had been one of the company's strengths, began to deteriorate, and productivity was compromised as a result.

Tom's withdrawal and Olivia's increasingly controlling behavior created a toxic work environment, where communication broke down, and trust was eroded. The team struggled to align on project priorities, as Tom's avoidance of group discussions left gaps in important project details. Olivia's insistence on adherence to the new system without understanding Tom's attachment needs led to further disengagement from Tom and made it more difficult for him to contribute effectively to the team.

Points of Analysis:

1. **Tom's dismissive-avoidant attachment style** is at the core of the conflict. His preference for autonomy and avoidance of relational interactions made it difficult for him to engage with Olivia's leadership style and the team's collaborative approach.

2. **Olivia's leadership style** is influenced by her need for control and structure. Her push for uniformity and her failure to consider Tom's attachment needs created a power struggle that intensified the conflict.

3. **The lack of emotional understanding and flexibility** from both Olivia and Tom exacerbated the situation. Olivia's inability to empathize with Tom's need for independence, and Tom's avoidance of addressing the issue directly, led to communication breakdowns and mutual frustration.

4. **The impact on the team:** The ongoing tension between Olivia and Tom divided the team, diminishing their ability to collaborate effectively and decreasing overall morale.

Possible Solutions:

- **Olivia's development of emotional intelligence:** Olivia could benefit from learning to recognize the different attachment styles within her team. By becoming more attuned to Tom's need for autonomy and adapting her leadership style to offer more flexibility, Olivia could create a more supportive and collaborative environment.
- **Supporting Tom's emotional needs:** Tom could be provided with opportunities for one-on-one conversations with Olivia, where he feels his concerns are heard and respected. Giving him space to express his thoughts without feeling judged could help him engage more fully with the team.
- **Improving team communication:** Encouraging open dialogue between team members about their preferences and

needs for collaboration can foster greater understanding and reduce tensions. Creating a culture of mutual respect for different working styles would allow both Olivia and Tom to find common ground.

Case Study 5: Tension Between a Senior Executive and a Junior Employee with an Anxious Attachment Style

Professional Context:
In a fast-growing tech company in San Francisco, the team of 30 employees is highly diverse, with members from different backgrounds and varying levels of experience. The company culture emphasizes innovation, agility, and a flat hierarchy, where all employees are encouraged to contribute ideas and collaborate across departments. The team is led by Caroline, a senior executive who has been with the company since its inception and has helped drive its expansion. Caroline is known for her strong leadership and ambition, but she is also highly demanding and results-oriented.

One of Caroline's junior employees, Emily, has been with the company for six months and has recently been promoted to a junior project manager role. Emily is highly motivated and eager to prove herself, but she has an anxious attachment style. She tends to seek validation from others and experiences significant distress when she feels uncertain about her performance or when her contributions are not acknowledged. Emily's anxiety often manifests in her seeking frequent feedback, reassurance, and approval, which can sometimes come across as overly eager or needy.

The Conflict:
The conflict between Caroline and Emily began when Emily was tasked with leading a project that required coordinating with multiple departments. Caroline, who typically takes a hands-off approach with her team but expects high performance, gave Emily the autonomy to manage the project but did not provide much guidance or feedback along the way. Emily, feeling insecure about her new responsibilities, sought frequent check-ins with Caroline to ensure that she was on the right track. However, Caroline, overwhelmed with her own responsibilities, did not have time for these check-ins and often

responded to Emily's emails or requests for meetings with brief, task-focused answers.

Feeling increasingly unsupported and anxious, Emily started to worry that she was failing to meet expectations. Her anxiety escalated as she began to doubt her decisions, constantly second-guessing herself and fearing that Caroline would disapprove of her work. Emily's anxiety led her to send Caroline more emails and schedule more meetings, hoping to receive validation and feedback. Caroline, meanwhile, became frustrated with what she perceived as a lack of confidence in Emily's abilities. She felt that Emily should be more independent and capable of managing the project without constant reassurance.

As the project deadline approached, the tension between Caroline and Emily reached a peak. Caroline became more critical of Emily's work, pointing out small errors and expressing dissatisfaction with the pace of the project. Emily, already overwhelmed by her anxiety, took this feedback very personally and became emotionally distressed. She started to withdraw from the team, unable to focus on the project due to her heightened anxiety. The emotional distance between Caroline and Emily made communication even more strained, and the project began to fall behind schedule.

The Impact on the Team:
The conflict between Caroline and Emily had a significant impact on the broader team. Other team members noticed the growing tension between the two and began to feel uncomfortable in their interactions with Emily, sensing her anxiety and withdrawal. Some colleagues tried to step in and offer support, but the overall atmosphere became more tense and fragmented. The lack of clear communication between Caroline and Emily also affected the project's progress, as team members received unclear instructions or had to wait for Emily to regain her focus before moving forward.

The team's morale suffered as a result of the conflict. Emily, once highly motivated and eager to contribute, became increasingly disengaged and unsure of how to approach her work. Caroline, focused on meeting deadlines and delivering results, did not recognize the emotional strain that Emily was under and continued to push for performance without providing the emotional support that Emily needed.

Points of Analysis:

1. **Emily's anxious attachment style** is central to the conflict. Her need for constant validation and feedback, coupled with her fear of failure, led to her seeking reassurance from Caroline. However, Caroline's lack of emotional responsiveness only increased Emily's anxiety, making her more dependent and disengaged.

2. **Caroline's leadership style**, focused on results and independence, created a mismatch with Emily's emotional needs. Caroline's tendency to prioritize task completion over emotional support left Emily feeling unsupported and uncertain, which only exacerbated the conflict.

3. **The lack of emotional support and clear communication** between Caroline and Emily intensified the situation. Caroline's frustration with Emily's perceived lack of confidence and Emily's emotional withdrawal created a cycle of miscommunication and resentment.

4. **The impact on the team:** The conflict between Caroline and Emily disrupted team dynamics, making it difficult for other team members to collaborate effectively. The tension between the two leaders also created uncertainty, as others were unsure how to navigate the emotional climate.

Possible Solutions:

- **Caroline's leadership adaptation:** Caroline could benefit from learning to recognize the emotional needs of her team, particularly employees with anxious attachment styles. Offering regular check-ins, positive reinforcement, and

reassurance could help Emily feel more secure in her role and reduce her anxiety.
- **Supporting Emily's emotional regulation:** Emily could benefit from coaching or mentoring to help her manage her anxiety and build confidence in her abilities. Learning to self-validate and cope with uncertainty would allow her to approach challenges with more resilience.
- **Improving team communication:** The team could benefit from a more structured approach to communication, with regular team meetings to discuss progress and address any concerns. Creating an environment where feedback is given constructively and empathetically would help foster trust and reduce anxiety.

Case Study 6: Conflict Between a Senior Manager and an Avoidantly Attached Employee

Professional Context:
In a large law firm based in Chicago, the team consists of 20 employees working across various departments, including litigation, corporate law, and client relations. The firm has a competitive and high-pressure environment, with demanding clients and tight deadlines. The senior manager, James, has been with the firm for over 15 years and is known for his strategic thinking and high expectations. James is a highly skilled manager but is focused more on results and efficiency than on fostering emotional connections within the team.

One of James' employees, Sarah, has been with the firm for three years. She is a senior associate in the corporate law department and is highly skilled at her job, consistently delivering high-quality work. However, Sarah has an avoidant attachment style. She tends to withdraw from emotionally charged situations, avoids conflict, and prefers to handle tasks independently. While Sarah is competent and reliable, she often resists team-building activities and avoids deep interpersonal engagements, especially when she feels her autonomy is being threatened.

The Conflict:
The conflict began when James, seeking to improve the performance of his team, decided to implement regular team meetings to discuss ongoing projects, share feedback, and foster more collaboration. He introduced the idea of weekly catch-up meetings, where each team member would present their progress and discuss any challenges they were facing. While the idea was meant to improve communication and team cohesion, Sarah found these meetings intrusive and counterproductive.

Sarah, accustomed to working autonomously, felt that these meetings undermined her independence. She did not see the need to share details of her work in a group setting, as she preferred to focus on tasks without external involvement. Despite her reservations, Sarah participated in the meetings, but her disengagement was apparent. She would provide short, task-focused updates, avoiding any personal or collaborative discussions. James, who valued open communication and teamwork, began to perceive Sarah's behavior as a lack of commitment and team spirit. He felt that her reluctance to engage was hindering the team's progress and undermining the collaborative culture he was trying to build.

Over time, James became increasingly frustrated with Sarah's resistance to the team meetings. He began to see her lack of participation as a challenge to his authority and the firm's values. Sarah, on the other hand, felt suffocated by the increased pressure to collaborate and engage emotionally with her colleagues. She began withdrawing further, both from meetings and from day-to-day interactions with her team. This led to a noticeable decline in the quality of communication within the team, and several colleagues began to express concerns about the lack of cohesion.

The Impact on the Team:
The tension between James and Sarah had a ripple effect on the team. Sarah's disengagement in meetings made it difficult for others to collaborate with her effectively, leading to a lack of clarity on certain projects. Her colleagues began to feel frustrated, as they were unable to get the input they needed from her. Some team members tried to engage her in private, but Sarah, feeling pressured, would shut down the conversations or redirect them to work-related matters only.

James, frustrated with Sarah's behavior, became more focused on ensuring that she participated in meetings, which only led to more conflict. He started assigning her tasks that required more direct collaboration with others, but Sarah's resistance to these collaborative efforts created friction and a sense of discomfort within the team. The overall atmosphere in the office became tense, and employees began to question whether the firm's culture of collaboration was truly inclusive or whether certain individuals were being pushed into uncomfortable situations.

Points of Analysis:

1. **Sarah's avoidant attachment style** is at the core of the conflict. Her preference for independence and avoidance of emotional engagement made it difficult for her to embrace the collaborative approach that James was trying to instill. Her discomfort with the team meetings and her emotional withdrawal created friction with the rest of the team.

2. **James' leadership style**, focused on driving collaboration and engagement, created a mismatch with Sarah's emotional needs. His insistence on team involvement without considering Sarah's need for autonomy exacerbated the conflict, leading to frustration and disengagement on both sides.

3. **The lack of understanding of attachment dynamics** contributed to the conflict. James did not recognize that Sarah's resistance was rooted in her attachment style and not a lack of commitment or professionalism. This miscommunication prevented both parties from addressing the real issue effectively.

4. **The impact on the team:** The conflict led to a breakdown in communication and collaboration within the team. Sarah's withdrawal created uncertainty and frustration among her colleagues, undermining the firm's goal of fostering a collaborative environment.

Possible Solutions:

- **James' emotional intelligence and adaptability:** James could benefit from learning about the different attachment styles within his team and adjusting his leadership approach accordingly. Recognizing that Sarah's need for independence is not a personal challenge to his authority could help him provide her with the space she needs to perform at her best while also encouraging her to participate in team efforts in ways that feel comfortable to her.

- **Supporting Sarah's autonomy:** Sarah could be given more opportunities to work independently while still being integrated into the team's overall goals. One-on-one meetings with James or a mentor could allow her to express her concerns and needs in a more controlled, less emotional setting, helping to bridge the gap between her need for independence and the firm's collaborative culture.
- **Creating a balanced approach to teamwork:** The firm could benefit from introducing flexible collaboration strategies that respect individual working styles. For example, Sarah could be invited to contribute to team discussions asynchronously (via email or collaborative platforms) rather than being pressured into regular meetings that feel intrusive. This could help create a balance between collaboration and autonomy, allowing for greater engagement from employees with avoidant attachment styles.

Case Study 7: Conflict Between a Manager and an Employee with a Secure Attachment Style

Professional Context:
In a well-established marketing agency in Los Angeles, the team consists of 25 employees working in diverse roles, including creative, client management, and analytics. The company has a collaborative and supportive culture, encouraging open communication and feedback across all levels. The team is led by a senior manager, Rachel, who has been with the agency for over a decade and is known for her dedication and strong leadership skills. Rachel is an experienced manager with a tendency to be somewhat controlling, often overseeing all aspects of the projects and expecting high levels of participation from her team.

James, one of Rachel's team members, has been with the agency for four years. James is an experienced creative strategist who excels in generating innovative ideas for campaigns. He has a secure attachment style, characterized by a balanced approach to relationships and a high level of emotional stability. James is confident in his abilities, comfortable with feedback, and values collaboration, but he also enjoys autonomy and the freedom to approach tasks in his own way. He has a healthy sense of independence but is equally comfortable working closely with others when needed.

The Conflict:
The conflict began when Rachel introduced a new initiative aimed at streamlining the team's workflow and improving project tracking. As part of this initiative, she required all team members to log their work into a central project management system daily, ensuring that every task, communication, and update was recorded. While the system was meant to improve transparency and accountability, James, who values a degree of autonomy in his creative process, found the new system restrictive. He felt that it infringed on his ability to manage his own time and ideas without excessive oversight.

James initially tried to accommodate Rachel's new system, but he quickly became frustrated with the time-consuming nature of the daily logging and the pressure it put on his creative process. He expressed his concerns to Rachel, explaining that the constant logging of tasks disrupted his flow and made him feel micromanaged. Rachel, however, viewed his feedback as resistance to change and interpreted it as a lack of commitment to the team's goals. She dismissed his concerns, believing that the new system would ultimately improve the team's productivity and that all team members needed to adapt to it.

The tension grew when Rachel continued to insist on the system's importance and demanded that James comply with the daily updates. James, feeling undermined and controlled, became more reluctant to engage fully with the system and started to pull back emotionally from Rachel's directives. This led to a subtle breakdown in communication, as James' frustration grew while Rachel's insistence on the new procedures intensified. James, typically communicative and open, began to avoid one-on-one meetings with Rachel, finding excuses to handle his work independently without needing to explain every detail.

The Impact on the Team:
The conflict between Rachel and James started to affect the wider team. While Rachel was focused on enforcing the new system across the board, the team's overall morale began to dip. James' reluctance to engage with the new initiative was noticeable to his colleagues, and some began to question the necessity of the new processes. The team had previously been highly collaborative, but the conflict between Rachel and James created an atmosphere of division, with some members siding with Rachel's view of maintaining structure and accountability, while others sympathized with James' desire for more independence and creative freedom.

The emotional tension between Rachel and James also led to decreased productivity, as James felt increasingly disengaged and demotivated by the constant pressure. The collaborative spirit of the team started to erode, as individuals became more focused on following the rules rather than contributing freely to the creative process. Even though James was not an overtly confrontational individual, his emotional withdrawal and reluctance to engage in meetings with Rachel created an undercurrent of dissatisfaction that affected the team's cohesiveness.

Points of Analysis:

1. **James' secure attachment style** is an important factor in the conflict. He values both independence and collaboration, but his frustration arose from the perceived micromanagement and excessive control over his work process. His secure attachment allows him to express his concerns openly, but Rachel's dismissive response to his needs created a misalignment between them.

2. **Rachel's leadership style**, which tends toward being directive and focused on control, clashed with James' preference for autonomy. While Rachel's intentions were to improve team efficiency, her failure to recognize the emotional and professional needs of her team members created resistance, especially in a highly skilled and confident individual like James.

3. **Lack of emotional awareness and flexibility** from Rachel led to a misunderstanding of James' attachment needs. While James communicated his concerns respectfully, Rachel's response was more focused on compliance than on emotional connection, which escalated the conflict.

4. **The impact on the team:** The conflict undermined the collaborative culture of the agency, creating divisions and affecting team morale. The emphasis on the system over emotional and professional needs led to decreased motivation and disengagement from key team members like James.

Possible Solutions:

- **Rachel's adaptability and emotional awareness:** Rachel could benefit from learning to recognize and accommodate

different working styles, particularly when managing employees with a secure attachment style who value autonomy. A more flexible approach to project management, with respect for personal working preferences, would help prevent similar conflicts in the future.
- **Supporting James' need for autonomy:** James could be given more space to manage his work in a way that aligns with his preferences. Providing more flexible check-ins and allowing him to maintain his creative process without excessive oversight would help him feel more engaged and motivated.
- **Fostering team cohesion through mutual understanding:** The team could benefit from a more open discussion of the new system, where individual needs and concerns are addressed. This could help Rachel understand the diverse attachment needs of her team members and adjust her approach accordingly to ensure that both team structure and autonomy are balanced.

Case Study 8: Tension Between a Junior Manager and an Employee with an Avoidant Attachment Style

Professional Context:
In a medium-sized consulting firm in Toronto, the team is made up of consultants, analysts, and support staff, all working together on large-scale projects for corporate clients. The company prides itself on its collaborative culture, with a focus on team-driven problem-solving and innovation. Emily, a junior manager in the company, was recently promoted after demonstrating strong performance in her consulting role. While she is a competent and enthusiastic manager, she is still adapting to her new leadership responsibilities.

One of her team members, Alex, is a senior consultant with over ten years of experience in the industry. Alex has an avoidant attachment style and values independence in his work. He is highly skilled and self-sufficient, preferring to work on his tasks alone and avoiding unnecessary collaboration or emotional engagement. Alex has always been an asset to the firm due to his expertise and ability to handle complex projects with minimal oversight. However, his attachment style makes it difficult for him to connect with others emotionally or participate in team-building activities, which has started to create tension in his relationship with Emily.

The Conflict:
The conflict between Emily and Alex began when Emily was tasked with managing a new client project. Emily's management style is collaborative and she believes in the power of team cohesion to solve problems and generate ideas. She scheduled frequent meetings for the team to discuss project progress, brainstorm solutions, and address challenges together. However, Alex, who prefers to work independently, felt that these meetings were a waste of time and disrupted his workflow. He began to disengage from the group

discussions, contributing little to the team's brainstorming sessions and avoiding meetings whenever possible.

Emily, noticing Alex's resistance, attempted to engage him in one-on-one conversations to better understand his concerns. However, Alex's avoidant attachment style caused him to withdraw even further. He downplayed his reasons for disengaging, stating that he simply preferred to focus on his individual tasks and didn't see the value in collaborative discussions. Emily, frustrated by Alex's lack of cooperation, began to see his behavior as insubordination and felt that he was not fully committed to the team's success. She tried to push him harder to participate in meetings and communicate more openly, but this only exacerbated Alex's discomfort, making him more resistant and distant.

As the project deadline loomed, the tension between Emily and Alex grew. Emily's need for open communication and regular updates clashed with Alex's desire for autonomy. Alex's refusal to engage in the group process led to a breakdown in communication within the team, as Emily struggled to get the information she needed from him. The lack of collaboration started to affect the project's progress, and Emily became increasingly frustrated, perceiving Alex's behavior as a personal challenge to her authority.

The Impact on the Team:
The conflict between Emily and Alex had a noticeable impact on the team's overall performance. While Emily tried to facilitate collaboration, Alex's reluctance to participate led to delays in decision-making and confusion within the team. Other team members began to notice the strain between their manager and Alex, and some started to feel uncomfortable participating in the group discussions, fearing further conflict. The project, which had the potential to be highly successful, began to stagnate due to the lack of alignment between the team members.

Emily's leadership was also called into question, as some team members felt that she wasn't effectively managing the situation with

Alex. They noticed that she was becoming more directive and less empathetic in her approach, and this led to a shift in the team dynamics. Some employees, sensing the increasing tension, began to withdraw emotionally as well, unsure how to address the growing friction.

Points of Analysis:

1. **Alex's avoidant attachment style** is a key factor in the conflict. His discomfort with emotional engagement and preference for independence led him to resist Emily's collaborative approach, which was central to her management style. His tendency to withdraw when faced with relational demands exacerbated the tension.

2. **Emily's leadership style**, while collaborative and inclusive, did not align well with Alex's emotional needs. Her insistence on frequent meetings and constant communication was perceived as intrusive by Alex, leading to his emotional withdrawal and resistance.

3. **Misunderstanding of attachment dynamics** led to a lack of empathy on both sides. Emily's frustration with Alex's resistance to collaboration clouded her ability to recognize the emotional needs driving his behavior. Similarly, Alex's discomfort with teamwork was exacerbated by Emily's increased pressure.

4. **The impact on the team:** The conflict not only affected Emily and Alex but also started to influence the rest of the team. The breakdown in communication and the growing emotional distance created a tense atmosphere that undermined team cohesion and productivity.

Possible Solutions:

- **Emily's adaptability in leadership:** Emily could benefit from learning more about attachment theory and how it impacts team dynamics. By understanding Alex's avoidant attachment style, she could adjust her leadership approach, offering more autonomy while still encouraging communication. Providing Alex with a clear rationale for team collaboration and allowing him space to contribute in a way that feels comfortable to him would help reduce the tension.

- **Supporting Alex's emotional needs:** Alex may benefit from one-on-one sessions with Emily or a mentor where he can express his concerns in a less intimidating, more controlled environment. Encouraging him to voice his discomfort with the collaborative process and helping him find ways to engage without feeling overwhelmed would foster better communication.
- **Building a balanced team culture:** The team as a whole could benefit from a discussion about different working styles and preferences. Creating a culture of mutual understanding, where both collaboration and independence are valued, would help prevent future conflicts and enhance overall team cohesion.

Case Study 9: Conflict Between a Senior Executive and a Junior Employee with a Disorganized Attachment Style

Professional Context:
In a large healthcare organization in Boston, the team consists of professionals from diverse backgrounds, including doctors, nurses, administrative staff, and management. The organization operates in a high-pressure environment, with strict regulatory requirements and a focus on providing excellent patient care. The team is led by a senior executive, Mark, who has been with the organization for over 20 years and has worked his way up from clinical roles to his current leadership position. Mark is a results-oriented leader who is highly focused on meeting goals, improving performance, and maintaining operational efficiency.

Jessica, one of the junior employees, is a recent graduate who has joined the healthcare organization as a support coordinator. She is highly capable but struggles with emotional regulation and interpersonal relationships due to her disorganized attachment style. Jessica's behavior can be unpredictable at times, with fluctuating reactions to feedback and an apparent difficulty in navigating workplace relationships. While she performs well in tasks that require technical skills, her emotional responses to stress and conflict can be erratic, leading to challenges in working closely with others.

The Conflict:
The conflict between Mark and Jessica began when Mark assigned Jessica a critical role in a new project aimed at improving patient care procedures. The project required Jessica to collaborate with multiple departments, ensuring that communication was clear and that all deadlines were met. Initially, Jessica was enthusiastic about the project and committed to making a positive impact. However, as the project progressed, Jessica began to feel overwhelmed by the demands of the

role. She started missing deadlines and failing to follow up with colleagues, leading to delays and confusion.

Mark, noticing the lack of progress, became frustrated with Jessica's performance and began to apply more pressure to ensure that tasks were completed on time. He scheduled frequent check-ins, expecting Jessica to provide updates and demonstrate progress. Jessica, however, felt increasingly anxious and out of control, especially when Mark began to raise concerns about her performance in front of the team. Her disorganized attachment style led her to feel both overwhelmed and fearful of Mark's criticism. At times, she would respond by becoming defensive or shutting down completely, which only exacerbated the situation.

One day, during a team meeting, Mark pointed out several mistakes that Jessica had made in her project coordination, publicly reprimanding her for not following through on her responsibilities. Jessica, already on edge, reacted by emotionally distancing herself from the team, and later that day, she sent an email to Mark expressing her frustration and accusing him of not supporting her when she needed help. This confrontation created a rift between them, as Mark felt that Jessica was being overly sensitive and unwilling to take constructive feedback.

The Impact on the Team:
The ongoing tension between Mark and Jessica began to affect the wider team. Colleagues who had initially been supportive of Jessica's role in the project became uncertain about how to interact with her. They noticed her emotional withdrawal and defensive behavior, which made collaboration difficult. The emotional climate within the team shifted, as some team members began to feel uncomfortable offering support to Jessica, fearing further conflict.

Meanwhile, Mark's frustration with Jessica's behavior made him more focused on achieving results rather than addressing the emotional needs of the team. His approach, which prioritized task completion over emotional engagement, led to a lack of empathy for Jessica's struggles. This created an unspoken divide between leadership and staff, making it harder for Jessica to find the support she needed. The project began to suffer from delayed decisions, poor communication, and a breakdown in teamwork.

Points of Analysis:

1. **Jessica's disorganized attachment style** is the root cause of the conflict. Her unpredictable emotional responses, which oscillate between defensive behavior and withdrawal, made it difficult for her to engage constructively with Mark's feedback. Disorganized attachment often manifests in erratic behavior under stress, which can lead to difficulties in navigating professional relationships.

2. **Mark's leadership style** is focused on efficiency and results, with little consideration for the emotional needs of his team members. His response to Jessica's difficulties—more pressure and public criticism—did not take into account her attachment needs. Mark's failure to address Jessica's emotional distress exacerbated her disengagement and resistance.

3. **The lack of emotional support and empathy** from both sides led to a breakdown in communication. Mark's feedback, which was intended to motivate Jessica, instead triggered her anxiety and defensiveness. Jessica's emotional responses created further distance, making it difficult for the two to have a productive conversation about the issues at hand.

4. **The impact on the team:** The conflict between Mark and Jessica created an atmosphere of discomfort and disengagement within the team. The emotional withdrawal and tension between leadership and staff affected the overall morale and collaboration, leading to delays and decreased productivity.

Possible Solutions:

- **Mark's emotional intelligence training:** Mark could benefit from learning about attachment theory and how different attachment styles impact workplace behavior. By understanding Jessica's disorganized attachment style, he could approach her with more empathy and patience, offering support rather than criticism when challenges arise.
- **Supporting Jessica's emotional regulation:** Jessica could benefit from mentorship or counseling to help her manage her anxiety and emotional reactions in stressful situations. Providing her with a safe space to express her concerns without fear of criticism would help her feel more secure and engaged in her work.
- **Team-building activities focused on emotional safety:** The team could benefit from training that helps improve communication and emotional awareness. By fostering a culture of mutual support and understanding, the team can learn to navigate conflicts more constructively and build stronger working relationships.

Case Study 10: Conflict Between a Project Manager and a Highly Autonomous Employee

Professional Context:
In a large advertising agency in Chicago, the team is composed of creative designers, account managers, and support staff working collaboratively to deliver high-profile campaigns for major brands. The agency is known for its innovative approach and dynamic environment, where employees are encouraged to take ownership of their work and contribute ideas. The team is led by Olivia, a project manager who has been with the company for over five years and has steadily risen through the ranks due to her strong organizational skills and focus on client relationships.

One of her team members, Richard, is a senior creative director who has been with the agency for eight years. Richard is highly skilled in his craft and known for his independent thinking and innovative ideas. However, Richard has an avoidant attachment style. He tends to work best when given complete autonomy, preferring to make decisions on his own without external interference. Richard is capable of managing projects independently but resists collaboration or the need for constant feedback. He believes that his work speaks for itself and that his creative process is best left undisturbed by frequent check-ins or meetings.

The Conflict:
The conflict arose when Olivia, in her role as project manager, began overseeing a new campaign for a prestigious client. Olivia's approach was to ensure that the team had regular meetings and updates to track progress, provide feedback, and ensure alignment across the team. She scheduled frequent brainstorming sessions and check-ins with all team members, including Richard, to maintain consistency and meet the client's expectations.

Richard, however, felt that these frequent meetings and updates were unnecessary and disruptive to his creative process. He began to disengage during the meetings, offering minimal input and focusing solely on the tasks that he was assigned. Olivia noticed his lack of participation and attempted to address it in one-on-one meetings, expressing that she needed more collaboration and transparency from him. Richard, feeling micromanaged, began to push back, stating that he worked better without constant supervision and that his creative work didn't require regular feedback.

Olivia, frustrated by Richard's resistance and feeling that his lack of engagement was hindering the progress of the project, started to escalate the pressure. She asked him to be more involved in team discussions and to provide regular updates on his progress. Richard, feeling increasingly constrained and undervalued, became more withdrawn. He started missing meetings and communicating less frequently with Olivia and the rest of the team. His disengagement created tension not only between him and Olivia but also among other team members, who began to feel the strain of his resistance to teamwork.

The Impact on the Team:
The conflict between Olivia and Richard quickly began to affect the dynamics of the entire team. As Richard withdrew, the rest of the team was left in a difficult position, uncertain of how to proceed with their work without full collaboration from one of their key members. Some team members felt uncomfortable stepping in to manage Richard's tasks, as they weren't sure how to approach him or address his disengagement without creating further conflict. The regular meetings, which were meant to foster communication, became increasingly tense, as Richard's avoidance of participation created a sense of dissonance among the group.

The overall project timeline also began to slip, as Richard's lack of collaboration delayed certain aspects of the campaign. Olivia, now increasingly stressed by the situation, became more directive in her management, giving Richard less space to work independently. This only further alienated Richard, who felt that his autonomy was being undermined and that his professional expertise was not being valued. The team's morale began to suffer as a result, with several team members expressing frustration with the lack of cohesion and communication.

Points of Analysis:

1. **Richard's avoidant attachment style** is central to the conflict. His preference for autonomy and independence, coupled with his discomfort with frequent check-ins and feedback, made it difficult for him to engage with Olivia's collaborative management style. His withdrawal was a direct response to feeling micromanaged, and this led to a breakdown in communication with his manager and the team.

2. **Olivia's management style**, which focuses on structure, regular feedback, and team collaboration, clashed with Richard's need for independence. Her increasing pressure on Richard to participate more actively in team discussions and meetings exacerbated the conflict, as Richard felt that his creative process was being interrupted.

3. **The lack of alignment between Olivia's expectations and Richard's emotional needs** led to frustration on both sides. Olivia did not recognize that Richard's resistance was a result of his attachment style, and Richard failed to communicate the emotional need behind his withdrawal. This lack of understanding created further tension.

4. **The impact on the team:** The conflict negatively affected team collaboration and morale. Richard's disengagement and Olivia's increased pressure created an environment where communication broke down, and the team struggled to meet deadlines and maintain a sense of unity.

Possible Solutions:

- **Olivia's leadership adaptation:** Olivia could benefit from recognizing that not all employees thrive in the same working environment. By offering Richard more autonomy and reducing the frequency of check-ins, she could help him feel more comfortable while still maintaining progress on the project. Having structured one-on-one meetings to discuss key decisions and feedback would provide Richard with the space he needs to work independently while keeping Olivia informed.
- **Supporting Richard's emotional needs:** Richard could benefit from coaching or mentorship to help him manage his resistance to collaboration and learn to express his concerns more constructively. By providing him with opportunities to share his perspective in a way that feels less intrusive, Olivia could help him feel more engaged in the team's efforts.
- **Fostering team cohesion and understanding:** The team could benefit from training on understanding different working styles and emotional needs. Creating a culture of respect for individuality while encouraging collaboration would allow for more productive teamwork, especially for employees like Richard who value autonomy but still need to be part of the collective process.

Case Study 11: Tension Between a Senior Executive and an Employee with an Anxious Attachment Style

Professional Context:
In a well-established financial services firm in New York City, the team is composed of analysts, associates, and senior executives working on high-stakes financial portfolios for institutional clients. The company values precision, accuracy, and attention to detail, making the work environment high-pressure and deadline-driven. The team is led by Robert, a senior executive who has been with the firm for over 15 years and is known for his rigorous approach to management and his expectations for excellence. While Robert is highly successful, he tends to be a bit distant and results-oriented, often prioritizing outcomes over team engagement.

One of Robert's employees, Laura, is an associate who has been with the firm for three years. Laura has a strong work ethic and consistently produces high-quality work. However, she has an anxious attachment style, characterized by a fear of abandonment and a strong need for validation. Laura is highly sensitive to feedback, and when she doesn't receive enough recognition or reassurance, she becomes anxious and uncertain about her performance. Her need for approval often manifests in seeking constant feedback and affirmation from her superiors, which can sometimes appear excessive or needy.

The Conflict:
The conflict began when Laura was assigned to a new project that required her to lead a team of analysts in preparing financial reports for a major client. Given the high visibility of the project, Robert was closely overseeing the work, and the team had to meet tight deadlines. Laura, as the project lead, felt a great deal of pressure to ensure everything was perfect. She began to seek regular feedback from Robert, asking if the reports were on the right track and requesting

input on minor details, even when the work was already aligned with expectations.

Robert, who was focused on managing multiple projects, began to see Laura's constant requests for validation as inefficient and unnecessary. He interpreted her behavior as a lack of confidence, which frustrated him. Robert's responses to Laura were often brief and to the point, telling her to "move forward" without offering the reassurance Laura was seeking. As the deadline approached, Laura's anxiety intensified, and she became more frequent in seeking Robert's feedback. She started emailing him multiple times a day for updates, even when there was no need for immediate response, fearing that any mistakes would reflect poorly on her.

Robert, perceiving Laura's behavior as micromanaging, became more frustrated and less responsive. He began to distance himself, communicating less frequently and offering curt feedback. Laura, feeling unsupported and insecure, became more anxious and began to second-guess her decisions. Her productivity started to decline as she spent more time worrying about the project's outcome and less time focusing on execution.

The Impact on the Team:
The conflict between Robert and Laura started to affect the rest of the team. Laura's anxiety created a tense atmosphere, as her frequent check-ins with Robert took up time that could have been spent on collaborative work. Some team members began to feel frustrated, as they were unsure how to respond to Laura's repeated requests for validation. They recognized that her need for reassurance was slowing down the process and creating delays, but they didn't feel comfortable addressing the issue directly.

As Robert withdrew emotionally, the team felt increasingly unsure of their standing on the project. Without clear feedback or guidance from Robert, team members became more focused on ensuring their work met expectations rather than contributing to the creative process. The lack of open communication led to confusion and uncertainty, reducing the overall efficiency of the team and diminishing morale. Laura, who had initially been a highly motivated employee, became increasingly disengaged, feeling unsupported and uncertain about her place in the team.

Points of Analysis:

1. **Laura's anxious attachment style** is central to the conflict. Her need for constant validation and reassurance, rooted in her attachment fears, caused her to seek feedback frequently, which Robert interpreted as a lack of confidence. This miscommunication exacerbated her anxiety, further distancing her from Robert.

2. **Robert's leadership style**, focused on results and efficiency, did not account for Laura's emotional needs. His tendency to minimize emotional engagement and prioritize outcomes left Laura feeling unsupported, which heightened her anxiety and decreased her productivity.

3. **The lack of emotional support and communication** led to a breakdown in their relationship. Robert's failure to recognize the emotional basis of Laura's behavior and Laura's inability to manage her anxiety created a cycle of miscommunication and frustration.

4. **The impact on the team:** The conflict between Robert and Laura created a tense working environment, slowing down productivity and eroding team morale. The lack of clear communication and emotional engagement between the two leaders left the team uncertain and disengaged.

Possible Solutions:

- **Robert's emotional intelligence training:** Robert could benefit from emotional intelligence training to better understand and manage employees' emotional needs, particularly those with anxious attachment styles. By offering

more reassurance and regular feedback, Robert could reduce Laura's anxiety and increase her confidence in her work.
- **Supporting Laura's emotional regulation:** Laura could benefit from mentoring or coaching to help her manage her attachment-driven anxieties and learn to self-validate. Providing her with tools to manage her emotional responses and encouraging her to seek feedback more strategically would improve her performance.
- **Improving team communication and support:** The team could benefit from more open communication about feedback and expectations. Regular team meetings, where feedback is shared in a constructive and supportive manner, would reduce anxiety and clarify team goals, improving collaboration and efficiency.

Case Study 12: Tension Between a Department Head and an Employee with a Secure Attachment Style

Professional Context:
In a global marketing firm based in London, the team is composed of 50 employees working across departments such as creative, content, data analytics, and client management. The company prides itself on its diverse and inclusive culture, with an emphasis on collaboration and professional growth. The head of the creative department, Jack, has been with the company for over 10 years and is a respected leader known for his innovative ideas and ability to motivate his team. However, Jack is highly results-oriented and has a tendency to push for high performance, often setting ambitious goals for his department.

One of Jack's employees, Claire, is a senior designer who has been with the firm for five years. Claire has a secure attachment style, characterized by emotional stability, confidence, and a healthy balance between independence and collaboration. Claire is highly motivated and works well both individually and in teams. She values feedback and feels comfortable engaging in both constructive discussions and brainstorming sessions. While she enjoys collaborating and contributing to team projects, she also values autonomy and prefers to have control over the direction of her work.

The Conflict:
The conflict began when Jack introduced a new initiative to the creative department: a series of ambitious campaigns for a high-profile client. Jack set aggressive timelines and expected all team members to work together seamlessly, frequently assigning new tasks and asking for updates in quick succession. While the initiative had great potential, the intensity of the workload began to cause stress within the team.

Claire, who typically thrives in environments where she has the freedom to explore her creative ideas, found herself struggling to keep up with the fast pace and the constant demand for updates. She began feeling overwhelmed by the pressure to meet Jack's high expectations, especially when he began to micromanage certain aspects of the design process, asking for multiple revisions on concepts that Claire felt were already strong. Claire's ability to manage her own workflow and make decisions autonomously was compromised by Jack's need for constant updates and changes, which left her feeling frustrated and less engaged with the project.

Claire expressed her concerns to Jack, explaining that the micromanaging and tight timelines were affecting her ability to work efficiently. She mentioned that she felt her design process was being interrupted by constant requests for revisions and that she needed more space to focus on her creative ideas. Jack, however, saw Claire's feedback as an indication that she wasn't fully committed to the project and that she was unable to handle the pressure. He believed that his high standards were necessary to ensure the success of the campaign and felt that Claire was resisting the push for perfection.

As Jack continued to push for more revisions and tighter deadlines, Claire became more disengaged, leading to a decline in the quality of her work. She started withdrawing from team meetings and becoming more reluctant to share her ideas. The emotional distance between Claire and Jack grew, and Jack began questioning whether Claire was the right fit for such a demanding project. Claire, feeling unsupported and misunderstood, began questioning her own abilities and became less confident in her work.

The Impact on the Team:
The tension between Claire and Jack started to affect the rest of the team. The other designers and creative professionals began to sense the discomfort between their department head and Claire. Some team members sided with Claire, feeling that the pace and pressure were unsustainable, while others felt that Jack's approach was necessary to deliver high-quality work. The division within the team led to a

decrease in collaboration, as employees were unsure whether they should follow Jack's directive style or support Claire's desire for more independence.

As the project continued, the lack of cohesion between Jack and Claire created an emotional divide within the team. Some employees began to feel disengaged, as they were caught between the two conflicting approaches. The pressure to deliver results led to increased stress across the department, reducing overall morale and affecting productivity.

Points of Analysis:

1. **Claire's secure attachment style** played a crucial role in the conflict. While she has emotional stability and can manage pressure well, her need for autonomy and her preference for working independently clashed with Jack's micromanagement and high-pressure environment. Her need for space to explore her creative process was not being met, which led to frustration and disengagement.

2. **Jack's leadership style**, which focuses on achieving high standards through control and frequent feedback, created a mismatch with Claire's attachment needs. While Jack's intentions were to push for excellence, his approach undermined Claire's ability to work autonomously, which impacted her performance and emotional engagement with the project.

3. **The lack of mutual understanding** between Jack and Claire was a key driver of the conflict. Jack did not recognize the importance of giving Claire the space and autonomy she needed to do her best work. Similarly, Claire's need for more independence was not communicated effectively, leading to a breakdown in their relationship.

4. **The impact on the team:** The conflict between Jack and Claire created division within the team, as members were

unsure how to navigate the competing demands for high performance and autonomy. The emotional distance between Jack and Claire affected team cohesion, reducing collaboration and lowering morale.

Possible Solutions:

- **Jack's adaptability in leadership:** Jack could benefit from understanding the attachment styles within his team and adapting his approach accordingly. By recognizing that Claire's secure attachment style allows her to work independently but also thrive with feedback, Jack could offer her more autonomy while still providing periodic check-ins and guidance. This would help create a more balanced environment where Claire feels both trusted and supported.
- **Supporting Claire's emotional needs:** Claire could benefit from more structured one-on-one meetings where she can voice her concerns without the pressure of constant revisions or feedback. By providing her with the space to express her creative ideas freely, Jack could help her regain confidence and ownership over her work.
- **Building a more collaborative team culture:** The team could benefit from discussing their working styles and establishing clear expectations about feedback, autonomy, and collaboration. By understanding and respecting each other's preferences, the team can work more cohesively, with a balance between individual autonomy and collective collaboration.

Case Study 13: Conflict Between a New Manager and a Long-Term Employee with an Avoidant Attachment Style

Professional Context:
In a fast-paced technology company based in Seattle, the team is composed of software engineers, data analysts, and project managers working on cutting-edge applications for the healthcare industry. The company is known for its innovative approach, and it values collaboration, agility, and creative problem-solving. The team is led by Sophie, a newly promoted manager who has been with the company for two years. Sophie is an ambitious and dynamic leader, focused on driving performance and ensuring that projects meet deadlines and exceed client expectations.

One of Sophie's team members, John, is a senior software engineer who has been with the company for seven years. John is highly skilled and has played a key role in the development of several successful products. However, John has an avoidant attachment style, which makes it difficult for him to engage in team discussions and collaborate openly with others. He prefers to work independently and often withdraws from interpersonal interactions, especially when emotions or group dynamics are involved. John is highly capable but tends to avoid situations that require emotional engagement or vulnerability.

The Conflict:
The conflict between Sophie and John began when Sophie was tasked with overseeing the development of a new software module that required collaboration between multiple departments, including engineering, design, and client services. Sophie, as a new manager, was eager to make a positive impression and sought to foster a collaborative team environment. She initiated weekly team meetings to discuss progress, address challenges, and ensure that everyone was aligned on project goals. These meetings were meant to promote

transparency, improve communication, and create a sense of camaraderie among team members.

John, however, found the meetings intrusive and unnecessary. He preferred to focus on his work without the constant interruptions of team discussions and status updates. His avoidance of group activities made it difficult for him to engage with the rest of the team during meetings, and he often provided minimal input when asked for feedback. Sophie, noticing John's withdrawal and lack of participation, began to express concern about his lack of engagement. She sent him several messages, encouraging him to speak up more during meetings and share his progress with the group.

John, feeling pressured and uncomfortable with the increased focus on collaboration, began to disengage even further. He started missing meetings and communicating less frequently with Sophie. Sophie, frustrated by what she perceived as John's lack of cooperation, became more insistent on getting regular updates and asked him to participate more actively in team discussions. John, feeling increasingly cornered, started to push back by refusing to attend certain meetings and working more independently without seeking feedback. His avoidance led to delays in the project, as other team members were left uncertain about his progress and the status of his contributions.

The Impact on the Team:
The conflict between Sophie and John began to affect the dynamics of the entire team. The other team members noticed that John was withdrawing from group activities, and some began to feel uncomfortable discussing project details without his input. The uncertainty about John's progress led to confusion and a lack of clarity regarding deadlines and project deliverables. Sophie's increased focus on ensuring that John participated in team activities put additional pressure on the rest of the team, who were caught between supporting Sophie's leadership and respecting John's need for autonomy.

As the tension grew, team morale started to suffer. Some team members began to take sides, with some supporting Sophie's emphasis on teamwork and collaboration, while others sympathized with John's need for space and independence. The lack of cohesion within the team led to inefficiencies in decision-making and a breakdown in communication. The emotional distance between Sophie and John created an atmosphere of discomfort, with both sides feeling frustrated and misunderstood. As a result, the overall productivity of the team decreased, and the project began to fall behind schedule.

Points of Analysis:

1. **John's avoidant attachment style** plays a significant role in the conflict. His preference for autonomy and emotional distance led him to withdraw from group activities and avoid emotional engagement with his manager and colleagues. His discomfort with collaboration created a rift between him and Sophie, which affected the team's overall performance.

2. **Sophie's leadership style**, focused on fostering teamwork and collaboration, did not align well with John's need for independence. Her emphasis on regular meetings and team check-ins, while well-intentioned, felt intrusive to John, which led to his disengagement and resistance.

3. **The lack of emotional understanding** from both Sophie and John contributed to the conflict. Sophie's insistence on collaboration and regular updates was perceived by John as a challenge to his autonomy, while John's withdrawal was seen by Sophie as a lack of commitment to the team.

4. **The impact on the team:** The tension between Sophie and John disrupted team cohesion, as members became uncertain about how to interact with John and how to manage the growing divide between their manager and a senior team member. The conflict also led to a decline in communication and collaboration, which impacted the project's progress.

Possible Solutions:

- **Sophie's leadership adaptation:** Sophie could benefit from understanding John's avoidant attachment style and adapting her leadership approach to respect his need for autonomy. Instead of pressuring John to attend all meetings, Sophie could provide him with more space to work independently while still maintaining clear channels of communication for project updates.
- **Supporting John's emotional needs:** John could benefit from one-on-one meetings with Sophie, where he can express his concerns and work through his discomfort with group dynamics. By giving him the opportunity to share his progress in a more private setting, Sophie could help him feel less pressured and more engaged in the project.
- **Improving team communication:** The team could benefit from a discussion about individual working preferences and how to balance autonomy with collaboration. By creating a culture of understanding and respect for different attachment styles, the team could find ways to improve communication and work more effectively together.

Case Study 14: Tension Between a Senior Consultant and a Junior Employee with a Secure Attachment Style

Professional Context:
In a well-established consulting firm based in Sydney, the team consists of a group of senior consultants, analysts, and junior associates. The firm specializes in providing strategic advice to large corporations in the finance sector. The environment is fast-paced, with tight deadlines and high client expectations. The team is led by a senior consultant, Daniel, who has been with the firm for over 15 years. Daniel is known for his expertise in financial analysis and his strong leadership, but he is also highly task-oriented and tends to focus primarily on results.

One of Daniel's junior employees, Sophie, has been with the firm for two years and has a secure attachment style. Sophie is competent, confident, and enjoys both working independently and collaborating with her colleagues. She values feedback, is comfortable with constructive criticism, and approaches her work with a balance of independence and teamwork. She enjoys contributing to group discussions but also values her space to work autonomously when necessary.

The Conflict:
The conflict began when Daniel was assigned to work with Sophie on a high-priority project that required the team to analyze and present financial strategies to a key client. As the project progressed, Daniel's approach to management began to clash with Sophie's working style. Daniel, who is results-driven, frequently checked in with Sophie to ensure that she was meeting milestones and deadlines. He would often suggest minor changes to Sophie's work, focusing on the small details rather than acknowledging the overall quality of the work Sophie had already done.

Sophie, who is confident in her ability to manage tasks and complete projects independently, began to feel micromanaged by Daniel. She had a clear idea of the direction she wanted to take with the project and preferred to work without constant interruptions. However, Daniel's frequent requests for updates and feedback led Sophie to feel that her expertise was being undermined. She began to feel frustrated by the constant scrutiny and started to withdraw emotionally, distancing herself from Daniel and becoming less communicative in meetings.

The situation came to a head when Daniel made a critical comment about one of Sophie's reports in front of the team, highlighting areas where she had missed details. Sophie, feeling embarrassed and unsupported, became defensive and asked to meet with Daniel privately to discuss her concerns. During the meeting, Sophie expressed that she felt her autonomy was being undermined and that her contributions were not being valued. Daniel, surprised by Sophie's emotional reaction, explained that he was simply trying to ensure that everything was perfect for the client. However, Sophie felt that Daniel's approach was overly critical and did not leave room for her to take ownership of her work.

The Impact on the Team:
The conflict between Daniel and Sophie began to affect the broader team. Other team members noticed the emotional distance between Sophie and Daniel and felt that the tension was affecting their ability to collaborate effectively. Some of the team members supported Sophie, recognizing that she had been given the freedom to work independently in the past and that her frustration was valid. Others, however, felt that Daniel's approach to leadership was necessary to maintain high standards and deliver results. The division between those who supported Sophie and those who sided with Daniel began to create a subtle rift within the team.

As Sophie withdrew emotionally, she began to feel less motivated to contribute her ideas and suggestions in team meetings. The overall productivity of the team suffered as a result, as the conflict between the two key players created a communication barrier. The project, which had initially been on track, began to experience delays as both Sophie and Daniel became more focused on their differences rather than working together toward a common goal.

Points of Analysis:

1. **Sophie's secure attachment style** allowed her to communicate her concerns with Daniel but also led to a sense of frustration when her emotional needs for autonomy and trust were not met. Her tendency to value independence in her work made her sensitive to Daniel's micromanaging approach, which led to disengagement.

2. **Daniel's leadership style**, focused on micromanaging and constant oversight, created a mismatch with Sophie's need for autonomy. While Daniel's intentions were to ensure quality and meet client expectations, his approach undermined Sophie's confidence and led to her emotional withdrawal.

3. **Miscommunication and lack of emotional sensitivity** contributed to the conflict. Daniel did not recognize that Sophie's need for space and independence was not a sign of disengagement but a reflection of her working style. Similarly, Sophie did not feel that Daniel understood the emotional toll that constant feedback was taking on her.

4. **The impact on the team:** The conflict between Daniel and Sophie created a divided team, with some members sympathizing with Sophie's desire for autonomy and others siding with Daniel's results-oriented approach. The lack of clear communication and mutual understanding diminished team cohesion and morale.

Possible Solutions:

- **Daniel's leadership adaptation:** Daniel could benefit from becoming more attuned to the attachment styles of his team members. By understanding that Sophie's secure attachment

style values both independence and feedback, Daniel could adjust his management style to allow her more autonomy while still providing periodic check-ins to ensure the project stays on track.
- **Supporting Sophie's emotional needs:** Sophie could be given more opportunities to take ownership of her work without constant interference. Allowing her to lead parts of the project independently, with less micromanagement, would help her feel more valued and engaged. One-on-one meetings with Daniel, where she can express her concerns without fear of criticism, could also improve communication.
- **Building team cohesion through open discussions:** The team could benefit from regular discussions about individual working styles and expectations. Encouraging open dialogue about how feedback is given and received would foster mutual understanding and allow team members to adapt to each other's preferences, improving overall collaboration.

Case Study 15: Conflict Between a New Manager and an Employee with a Dismissive-Avoidant Attachment Style

Professional Context:
In a fast-growing e-commerce company based in San Francisco, the team consists of marketing, logistics, customer service, and operations departments. The company is known for its innovative approach to online retail and its commitment to customer experience. The team is led by Laura, a newly promoted manager who has transitioned from a more hands-on role in customer service to overseeing a team of five employees in the operations department. While Laura is highly organized and results-driven, she is still adjusting to the nuances of leadership and managing diverse team members with varying emotional needs.

One of her team members, Greg, has been with the company for four years and is highly skilled in his role in logistics and operations. Greg is efficient, productive, and works well independently. However, Greg has a dismissive-avoidant attachment style, which makes him uncomfortable with emotional engagement and group interactions. He prefers to focus on tasks rather than relationships and is often resistant to collaborative team activities. While Greg is a strong performer, his attachment style leads him to avoid close interpersonal relationships and emotional discussions, especially with authority figures like Laura.

The Conflict:
The conflict between Laura and Greg began when Laura introduced a new initiative aimed at improving communication and collaboration within the team. She introduced weekly team meetings, where all team members were expected to share updates, discuss challenges, and engage in brainstorming sessions. Laura believed that the initiative would foster a sense of teamwork and improve overall productivity. However, Greg, who preferred working alone and avoided group

discussions, found the meetings intrusive and unnecessary. He felt that his work was being scrutinized unnecessarily and that the meetings were taking time away from his tasks.

Despite his discomfort, Greg attended the meetings, but his contributions were minimal. Laura noticed that Greg often seemed disengaged during the discussions, and his lack of participation frustrated her. She interpreted his behavior as a lack of interest in the team's goals and a failure to take responsibility for group collaboration. Laura attempted to engage Greg in one-on-one conversations to better understand his concerns, but Greg, uncomfortable with emotional discussions, became defensive and dismissed the need for additional meetings. He stated that he preferred to focus on his tasks and didn't need constant collaboration to perform his job effectively.

As the project progressed, Laura continued to push for more team involvement, encouraging Greg to contribute more actively. Greg, in turn, began to withdraw further, missing meetings and avoiding one-on-one check-ins with Laura. This created tension between them, as Laura became frustrated with Greg's resistance to teamwork and his perceived lack of commitment to the project. Greg, on the other hand, felt increasingly alienated and unsupported by Laura's demands for emotional engagement.

The Impact on the Team:
The ongoing conflict between Laura and Greg started to affect the team's overall dynamics. Other team members began to notice Greg's disengagement and his avoidance of group activities. Some employees began to feel uncomfortable around Greg, unsure how to interact with him, while others sympathized with his desire for autonomy. The lack of communication between Greg and Laura created confusion, as team members were unsure whether Greg was on track with the project or whether his resistance was causing delays.

Laura's continued focus on team collaboration created tension among other employees as well, as they felt caught between the need to meet

Laura's expectations and Greg's reluctance to participate. The emotional distance between Laura and Greg made it difficult for the rest of the team to feel confident in their progress, leading to a decline in morale and productivity. The team's cohesion weakened as a result, and their ability to work together efficiently was compromised.

Points of Analysis:

1. **Greg's dismissive-avoidant attachment style** is at the heart of the conflict. His preference for autonomy and avoidance of emotional engagement led him to resist the collaborative efforts initiated by Laura. His discomfort with interpersonal interactions, especially those that involve emotional content, made it difficult for him to connect with Laura and the rest of the team.

2. **Laura's leadership approach**, which focused on team collaboration and emotional engagement, clashed with Greg's need for independence. Her attempts to encourage participation and foster teamwork were perceived as intrusive by Greg, which led to emotional withdrawal and disengagement.

3. **Miscommunication and lack of empathy** were key factors in the conflict. Laura failed to recognize that Greg's resistance to team meetings was driven by his attachment style rather than a lack of commitment to the project. Similarly, Greg did not communicate the emotional impact of Laura's leadership approach on his ability to work effectively.

4. **The impact on the team:** The conflict disrupted the team's ability to collaborate and work efficiently. The tension between Laura and Greg created uncertainty, as other team members were unsure how to navigate the differing expectations around teamwork and individual autonomy.

Possible Solutions:

- **Laura's emotional intelligence development:** Laura could benefit from understanding Greg's dismissive-avoidant attachment style and adjusting her leadership approach accordingly. By providing Greg with more autonomy while still maintaining clear channels of communication, Laura could help him feel more comfortable and engaged in the project.
- **Supporting Greg's emotional needs:** Greg could benefit from more structured one-on-one meetings with Laura, where he can express his concerns in a low-pressure environment. Acknowledging his need for space and allowing him to work independently while still being part of the team could help him engage more fully.
- **Improving team communication:** The team could benefit from discussing individual preferences and expectations regarding collaboration. Creating an environment that respects both independence and teamwork would help mitigate future conflicts and improve overall team dynamics.

Case Study 16: Tension Between a Senior Executive and an Employee with a Fearful-Avoidant Attachment Style

Professional Context:
In a high-stakes advertising agency in Los Angeles, the team is composed of creative directors, copywriters, designers, and client-facing account managers. The agency is known for its fast-paced environment and its emphasis on creativity and client satisfaction. The team is led by William, a senior executive with over 20 years of experience in the industry. He is known for his strategic thinking and high expectations but struggles with emotional intelligence and managing interpersonal relationships. William values results above all and expects his team to meet tight deadlines and deliver innovative solutions to clients.

One of William's team members, Rachel, is a senior account manager who has been with the agency for five years. Rachel has a fearful-avoidant attachment style, which manifests as an internal conflict between a desire for connection and a fear of being rejected or criticized. While she values relationships with her colleagues, Rachel often struggles with feelings of insecurity and anxiety, particularly when it comes to receiving feedback or engaging in confrontational discussions. Her tendency to withdraw in the face of stress and her fear of rejection make it difficult for her to engage fully in the team's collaborative environment.

The Conflict:
The conflict began when Rachel was assigned to manage a high-profile campaign for a major client. The project required close collaboration between Rachel, the creative team, and the client, with frequent presentations and updates. Initially, Rachel was excited about the opportunity but soon began to feel overwhelmed by the pressure and the constant demands for perfection. William, who is highly results-driven, began to provide frequent, direct feedback on Rachel's

work. While his intentions were to improve the campaign, Rachel interpreted the feedback as personal criticism, which triggered her anxiety and fear of rejection.

Rachel began to withdraw emotionally, avoiding William's feedback and becoming defensive when he pointed out areas that needed improvement. William, frustrated by Rachel's lack of responsiveness, began to push harder, demanding more frequent updates and setting increasingly high expectations. Rachel, feeling both overwhelmed and unsupported, became more anxious and reluctant to engage in discussions. She began to miss deadlines, and her communication with William became more minimal and distant.

William, perceiving Rachel's withdrawal as a lack of commitment, began to question her abilities and her fit for the project. He became more critical and started to micromanage, asking for more frequent reports and setting stricter timelines. Rachel, feeling trapped and misunderstood, continued to withdraw, which further fueled William's frustration. As the conflict escalated, Rachel's work performance began to suffer, and her relationship with William deteriorated further.

The Impact on the Team:
The ongoing conflict between Rachel and William started to affect the broader team. Other team members noticed Rachel's emotional withdrawal and her reluctance to engage in group discussions. They were unsure how to approach her or offer support, given her defensiveness and tendency to shut down when feedback was offered. Some colleagues tried to step in and offer guidance, but Rachel's fear of criticism prevented her from accepting help.

Meanwhile, William's increasing frustration with Rachel began to affect his interactions with the rest of the team. His heightened focus on results and performance created a tense atmosphere, as employees felt they were constantly under pressure to meet expectations. The team's overall morale began to suffer, as the emotional distance between Rachel and William created an undercurrent of anxiety that affected everyone's ability to collaborate effectively.

The project, which was initially on track to be a success, began to experience delays and miscommunications. The lack of emotional support for Rachel, combined with William's escalating demands, led to a breakdown in communication and a decline in overall team performance. The emotional divide between Rachel and William created a toxic environment that stifled creativity and hindered progress.

Points of Analysis:

1. **Rachel's fearful-avoidant attachment style** plays a central role in the conflict. Her internal conflict between wanting to connect with others and fearing rejection led her to withdraw when faced with feedback or criticism. Her fear of failure and emotional vulnerability made it difficult for her to engage constructively with William's direct feedback, which exacerbated the situation.

2. **William's leadership style**, focused on results and performance, did not account for Rachel's emotional needs. His tendency to push for more frequent updates and his increasing micromanagement only heightened Rachel's anxiety and further distanced her emotionally. His lack of emotional intelligence made it difficult for him to see that Rachel's withdrawal was a response to his critical feedback rather than a lack of commitment.

3. **The lack of emotional support and empathy** from both Rachel and William contributed to the conflict. William's failure to recognize Rachel's need for positive reinforcement and emotional validation led to her disengagement. Rachel's inability to communicate her emotional needs and her fear of being rejected prevented her from seeking the support she needed.

4. **The impact on the team:** The conflict created a toxic environment, affecting the morale and productivity of the entire team. The emotional distance between Rachel and

William led to a breakdown in communication and collaboration, making it difficult for the team to stay aligned on project goals and timelines.

Possible Solutions:

- **William's emotional intelligence development:** William could benefit from understanding the attachment styles within his team and adapting his leadership approach accordingly. By recognizing Rachel's fearful-avoidant attachment style, he could offer more positive reinforcement and reassurance, while also providing her with the space to work independently. This would help reduce Rachel's anxiety and increase her engagement in the project.
- **Supporting Rachel's emotional regulation:** Rachel could benefit from mentorship or coaching to help her manage her anxiety and improve her ability to accept constructive feedback. Offering her regular opportunities to express her concerns in a supportive, non-judgmental environment would help her feel more secure and confident in her role.
- **Creating a culture of empathy and support:** The team could benefit from regular check-ins and open discussions about emotional needs and feedback. By fostering a culture of mutual support and understanding, the team can work together more effectively and reduce the emotional strain that conflicts like this one can cause.

Bibliography

Books and Articles on Attachment Theory

Bowlby, J. (1969). *Attachment and Loss: Volume I: Attachment.* Basic Books.
This foundational text by John Bowlby, the father of attachment theory, outlines the concept of attachment, its evolutionary basis, and its importance in early child development. Bowlby's work is essential for understanding how attachment behaviors are formed and the long-term impact of early attachment experiences on adult relationships and professional behavior.

Bowlby, J. (1973). *Attachment and Loss: Volume II: Separation Anxiety and Anger.* Basic Books.
In this second volume, Bowlby explores the emotional responses associated with separation from attachment figures, a critical aspect of attachment theory. This work provides an understanding of the anxieties and conflicts that arise in relationships, offering insights relevant to conflict resolution in the workplace.

Bowlby, J. (1980). *Attachment and Loss: Volume III: Loss: Sadness and Depression.* Basic Books.
This third volume deepens the exploration of the impact of loss on attachment relationships, focusing on sadness and depression. It is particularly relevant for understanding the emotional reactions of employees in workplace settings when faced with loss, both personal and professional.

Ainsworth, M. D. S. (1979). *Attachment, Affectional Ties, and the Lifespan. American Psychologist,* 34(10), 1047-1055.
Mary Ainsworth's work on attachment patterns and her development of the Strange Situation procedure are essential for understanding how early attachment experiences shape adult relational behaviors. This article discusses the different attachment styles—secure, anxious, and avoidant—and their implications for relationships throughout life.

Main, M., & Solomon, J. (1986). *Disorganized/disoriented attachment and caregiving. Handbook of Infant Development*, 2, 1215-1250.
This work by Main and Solomon extends Ainsworth's attachment theory by introducing the concept of disorganized attachment, a key framework for understanding complex attachment behaviors. It is particularly important for understanding attachment-related behaviors in leaders and employees with insecure attachment styles, including those that manifest in unpredictable or disorganized responses.

Books on Emotional Intelligence and Leadership

Goleman, D. (1995). *Emotional Intelligence: Why It Can Matter More Than IQ*. Bantam.
Daniel Goleman's influential book on emotional intelligence (EI) is essential for understanding how emotional awareness and regulation influence leadership and interpersonal relationships in the workplace. Goleman's framework connects emotional intelligence with leadership effectiveness and team performance, providing tools for enhancing emotional safety and communication.

Goleman, D., Boyatzis, R., & McKee, A. (2002). *Primal Leadership: Unleashing the Power of Emotional Intelligence*. Harvard Business Review Press.
This book further explores the role of emotional intelligence in leadership, offering practical strategies for leaders to harness their emotional intelligence to inspire and motivate teams. It discusses how attachment-related behaviors influence leadership styles and team dynamics.

Salovey, P., & Mayer, J. D. (1990). *Emotional Intelligence. Imagination, Cognition and Personality*, 9(3), 185-211.
This seminal paper by Salovey and Mayer defines emotional intelligence as the ability to monitor one's own and others' emotions, differentiate among them, and use this information to guide thinking and behavior. Their framework is key for understanding how emotional intelligence contributes to effective leadership and conflict resolution in professional settings.

Books on Leadership and Organizational Culture

Edmondson, A. C. (1999). *Psychological Safety and Learning Behavior in Work Teams. Administrative Science Quarterly*, 44(2), 350-383.
Edmondson's research on psychological safety explores how teams can function at their best when members feel safe to take interpersonal risks. This is crucial for fostering emotionally safe environments in the workplace, aligning with attachment-informed leadership practices. It's essential for understanding how trust and relational security can enhance team dynamics and performance.

Kahn, W. A. (1990). *Psychological Conditions of Personal Engagement and Disengagement at Work. Academy of Management Journal*, 33(4), 692-724.
Kahn's work on the psychological conditions of engagement and disengagement is fundamental for understanding emotional safety in the workplace. He identifies how relational aspects of the work environment—such as trust, empathy, and emotional connection—are key factors that determine whether employees engage or withdraw. His work is particularly relevant for attachment theory in organizational settings.

Schein, E. H. (2010). *Organizational Culture and Leadership*. Jossey-Bass.
Schein's work on organizational culture and leadership offers a comprehensive framework for understanding how culture is shaped by leadership behaviors and relational dynamics. His insights into how leaders influence organizational culture are key for developing emotionally safe and inclusive work environments informed by attachment theory.

Books on Conflict Resolution and Workplace Communication

Deutsch, M. (1973). *The Resolution of Conflict: Constructive and Destructive Processes*. Yale University Press.
Deutsch's foundational work on conflict resolution discusses how conflicts can either be resolved constructively or destructively. His

theories on cooperation, competition, and conflict management align closely with attachment-informed practices, offering strategies to navigate workplace conflicts in ways that strengthen relationships rather than undermine them.

Fisher, R., Ury, W., & Patton, B. (2011). *Getting to Yes: Negotiating Agreement Without Giving In* (3rd ed.). Penguin Books.
This widely regarded text on negotiation provides valuable strategies for resolving conflicts by focusing on mutual gains rather than positional bargaining. Attachment theory plays a role here in understanding how people approach negotiation—whether with trust and openness (secure attachment) or defensiveness and suspicion (insecure attachment).

Bower, R. S., & Bower, M. S. (1998). *Conflict Resolution: A Practical Guide to Developing Negotiation Skills*. Palgrave Macmillan.
This practical guide offers tools for managing workplace conflicts, focusing on how to apply negotiation strategies in real-world situations. The book emphasizes the importance of emotional intelligence and relational understanding, which can be enhanced through attachment-informed approaches to leadership and communication.

Books and Articles on Diversity, Inclusion, and Organizational Behavior

Kramer, R. M. (1999). *Trust and Distrust in Organizations: Emerging Perspectives, Enduring Questions. Annual Review of Psychology,* 50, 569-598.
Kramer's work explores the dynamics of trust and distrust within organizations, a critical component of attachment theory. Understanding how attachment styles influence trust-building behaviors helps leaders create inclusive, emotionally safe work environments. His work is particularly valuable for exploring how relational dynamics can either enhance or hinder organizational effectiveness.

Shore, L. M., Cleveland, J. N., & Sanchez, D. (2018). *Inclusive Workplaces: A Review and Model. Human Resource Management Review*, 28(2), 176-189.

This article reviews the concept of inclusive workplaces, offering a model for integrating diversity and inclusion strategies into organizational culture. It emphasizes the importance of relational safety and fairness, which are foundational to attachment-informed leadership and organizational practices.

Roberson, Q. M. (2006). *Disentangling the Meanings of Diversity and Inclusion in Organizations. Group & Organization Management*, 31(2), 212-236.

Roberson examines how the terms "diversity" and "inclusion" are understood and applied within organizations. Her work sheds light on how attachment-informed practices can enhance inclusivity by addressing relational dynamics and promoting emotional safety for all employees.

Articles on Attachment and Workplace Relationships

Hazan, C., & Shaver, P. R. (1987). *Romantic Love Conceptualized as an Attachment Process. Journal of Personality and Social Psychology*, 52(3), 511-524.

This pioneering article by Hazan and Shaver applies attachment theory to adult romantic relationships, providing foundational insights into how attachment patterns influence adult interpersonal behavior. Their work has since been extended to understanding workplace relationships, particularly in terms of leadership, teamwork, and collaboration.

Mikulincer, M., & Shaver, P. R. (2016). *Attachment in Adulthood: Structure, Dynamics, and Change*. Guilford Press.

Mikulincer and Shaver's comprehensive book explores how attachment theory applies to adult relationships, including in workplace settings. It discusses how attachment styles influence leadership, conflict resolution, and collaboration, offering key insights for attachment-informed approaches to organizational behavior.

Books on Emotional Safety and Organizational Culture

Edmondson, A. C. (2018). *The Fearless Organization: Creating Psychological Safety in the Workplace for Learning, Innovation, and Growth*. Wiley.
Edmondson's book extends her earlier work on psychological safety, offering practical strategies for fostering environments where employees feel safe to take risks and speak up. This work is highly relevant for understanding the relational dynamics that create emotionally safe workspaces, which can be nurtured through attachment-informed leadership practices.

Kegan, R., & Lahey, L. L. (2009). *Immunity to Change: How to Overcome It and Unlock the Potential in Yourself and Your Organization*. Harvard Business Review Press.
Kegan and Lahey explore how individuals and organizations resist change, offering strategies for overcoming these barriers. Their work ties into attachment theory by addressing how fear of change and relational insecurity can hinder growth. By understanding these dynamics, leaders can create environments that support emotional safety and foster adaptive change.

Research on Organizational Behavior and Attachment Styles

Bowlby, J., & Ainsworth, M. D. S. (1972). *The Development of Attachment and Affiliative Systems*. Handbook of Child Psychology, 2, 37-66.
This classic work co-authored by Bowlby and Ainsworth lays the foundation for understanding how attachment systems develop in childhood and continue to influence behavior in adulthood. It's critical for understanding how attachment behaviors affect professional relationships and organizational dynamics.

Mikulincer, M., & Shaver, P. R. (2007). *Attachment in Adults: Clinical and Developmental Perspectives*. Guilford Press.
Mikulincer and Shaver's work explores the clinical and developmental aspects of attachment in adulthood. This book provides a detailed look at how attachment styles influence emotional regulation, leadership,

and interpersonal dynamics in the workplace. It is a key resource for applying attachment theory in professional environments.

Other Resources on Attachment Theory in Professional Contexts

Harms, P. D., & Crede, M. (2010). *Emotional Intelligence and Transformational and Transactional Leadership: A Meta-Analytic Review. Journal of Leadership & Organizational Studies*, 17(1), 5-18. This meta-analysis explores the relationship between emotional intelligence and leadership styles. It highlights the relevance of attachment theory in understanding how emotional intelligence shapes leadership effectiveness, particularly in fostering emotionally safe and inclusive work environments.

Popper, M., & Mayseless, O. (2003). *The Role of Attachment in Transformational Leadership. The Leadership Quarterly*, 14(1), 47-64. Popper and Mayseless examine the relationship between attachment and transformational leadership, offering insights into how leaders with secure attachment styles can inspire and motivate their teams. Their findings are key for understanding how attachment theory shapes leadership behaviors and organizational outcomes.

Table of content

Introduction: Understanding Attachment and Workplace Dynamics... .3
   Attachment Theory and Its Relevance in the Professional World...4
   The Role of Emotional Safety in Workplace Success..................... .5
   Bringing Attachment Theory into the Modern Workplace.............7
   Looking Ahead... .8

Chapter 1: What Is Attachment Theory?............................ .10
   The Foundations of Attachment Styles..11
   The Evolution of Attachment Theory..13
   The Science Behind Attachment in the Workplace...................... .15
   Implications for Leadership and Organizational Culture..............16
   The Foundation for a New Workplace Paradigm......................... .17

Chapter 2: Recognizing Attachment Styles at Work...........18
   The Power of Self-Awareness... .18
   Creating a Workplace Culture of Empathy and Understanding....21
   Practical Tools for Identifying Attachment Styles........................23
   The Benefits of Attachment-Informed Practices.......................... .24
   A Lens for Understanding Workplace Dynamics......................... .25

Chapter 3: The Role of Emotional Safety in Professional Relationships.. .26
   Attachment Theory and Emotional Safety................................... .27
   Building Trust Through Emotional Safety................................... .29
   Conflict Resolution and Emotional Safety....................................30
   The Transformative Power of Emotional Safety...........................32
   Emotional Safety as a Catalyst for Success...................................33

Chapter 4: Attachment Styles and Communication............34
   Secure Attachment and Effective Communication........................35
   Avoidant Attachment and the Struggle for Connection.................36
   Bridging Attachment Styles in Communication............................38
   Communication in High-Stress Scenarios.....................................40
   The Transformative Power of Attachment-Informed Communication.. .41

Chapter 5: Attachment Styles and Leadership.................... .42
   Secure Attachment and Effective Leadership...............................42
   Avoidant Attachment and Leadership Challenges........................44
   The Ripple Effects of Attachment-Informed Leadership..............46
   Leadership Styles and Organizational Outcomes......................... .47
   Redefining Leadership Through Attachment Theory................... .48

Chapter 6: Building Collaborative Relationships................49
   Trust: The Foundation of Collaboration..49

- Bridging Differences in Collaboration..51
- The Role of Feedback in Collaboration...53
- Practical Strategies for Collaborative Conflict Resolution...........55
- Collaboration as a Relational Skill..56

Chapter 7: Attachment Styles and Leadership Behaviors...57
- Secure Attachment: The Foundation of Relational Leadership.....58
- Avoidant Attachment: Leadership from a Distance.......................59
- Leadership Styles and Organizational Culture..............................61
- Practical Steps for Attachment-Informed Leadership....................63
- Transforming Leadership Through Attachment Theory................63

Chapter 8: Becoming an Emotionally Intelligent Leader....65
- The Foundations of Emotional Intelligence in Leadership...........65
- Practical Strategies for Self-Regulation..67
- Building Empathy as a Leadership Skill..69
- Practical Strategies for Enhancing Social Skills...........................71
- Emotional Intelligence as a Transformative Leadership Tool.......71

Chapter 9: Understanding Conflict Through the Lens of Attachment..73
- Attachment Styles and Their Impact on Conflict..........................73
- Disorganized Attachment and Conflict Dynamics........................76
- The Role of Emotional Regulation in Conflict Resolution...........77
- Fostering a Culture of Constructive Conflict................................79
- Conflict as an Opportunity for Growth...80

Chapter 10: Strategies for Managing and Resolving Workplace Conflicts...81
- Building a Foundation for Conflict Resolution.............................81
- Empathy and Active Listening in Conflict Resolution..................83
- Strategies for Supporting Emotional Regulation..........................85
- Conflict Resolution as a Relational Skill......................................87
- Building a Culture of Constructive Conflict.................................87

Chapter 11: Creating Inclusive and Emotionally Safe Work Environments..88
- The Role of Leadership in Fostering Inclusion and Safety...........89
- The Importance of Representation in Inclusion............................91
- Establishing Shared Values and Norms...92
- The Role of Leadership in Sustaining Culture..............................94
- Toward a More Inclusive and Relational Workplace....................94

Chapter 12: Measuring and Enhancing Emotional Safety in the Workplace..96
- The Relational Context of Emotional Safety................................96
- Assessing Emotional Safety in Teams...98
- Leveraging Technology to Enhance Emotional Safety...............100
- The Business Case for Emotional Safety....................................101
- Institutionalizing Emotional Safety...102

Conclusion: Attachment Theory and the Future of Work..103
   The Broader Implications of Emotional Safety............................104
   The Transformative Power of Relational Leadership...................105
   Attachment Theory in Remote and Hybrid Workplaces...............107
   A Vision for Relational Workplaces..109
   A Call to Action..109

Case Study 1: Conflict Between Leadership and an Anxiously Attached Employee.. .111

Case Study 2: Tension Between a Team Leader and an Avoidantly Attached Employee..114

Case Study 3: Disagreement Between a Senior Manager and a Disorganized-Attached Employee.................................. .117

Case Study 4: Tension Between a Young Manager and a Highly Independent Employee..121

Case Study 5: Tension Between a Senior Executive and a Junior Employee with an Anxious Attachment Style........125

Case Study 6: Conflict Between a Senior Manager and an Avoidantly Attached Employee..129

Case Study 7: Conflict Between a Manager and an Employee with a Secure Attachment Style........................133

Case Study 8: Tension Between a Junior Manager and an Employee with an Avoidant Attachment Style..................137

Case Study 9: Conflict Between a Senior Executive and a Junior Employee with a Disorganized Attachment Style..141

Case Study 10: Conflict Between a Project Manager and a Highly Autonomous Employee.. .145

Case Study 11: Tension Between a Senior Executive and an Employee with an Anxious Attachment Style...................149

Case Study 12: Tension Between a Department Head and an Employee with a Secure Attachment Style........................153

Case Study 13: Conflict Between a New Manager and a Long-Term Employee with an Avoidant Attachment Style .... .157

Case Study 14: Tension Between a Senior Consultant and a Junior Employee with a Secure Attachment Style............161

Case Study 15: Conflict Between a New Manager and an Employee with a Dismissive-Avoidant Attachment Style.165

Case Study 16: Tension Between a Senior Executive and an Employee with a Fearful-Avoidant Attachment Style.......169

Bibliography 173
Table of content 180